Communicating Online

Communicating Online
A Guide to the Internet

John A. Courtright
University of Delaware

Elizabeth M. Perse
University of Delaware

Mayfield Publishing Company
Mountain View, California
London • Toronto

Library of Congress Cataloging-in-Publication Data

Courtright, John A.
    Communicating online: a guide to the Internet / John A.
Courtright, Elizabeth M. Perse.
        p.   cm.
    Includes index.
    ISBN 0-7674-246-4
        1. Internet (Computer network) 2. Electronic mail systems.
    3. World Wide Web (Information retrieval system) I. Perse,
    Elizabeth M.   II. Title
    TK5101.875.I57C69 1997
    005.7' 1376--dc21

                                    97-31692
                                    CIP

Manufactured in the United States of America
10   9   8   7   6   5   4   3   2   1

Sponsoring editor, Holly Allen; production editor, Melissa Kreischer; manuscript editor, Jan deProsse; cover designer, Terri Wright; manufacturing manager, Tricia Reynolds. Cover photo © Alán Gallegos/A.G. Photograph. The text was set in 11/13 Palatino and printed on acid-free 50# Thor offset and printed by Malloy Lithographing, Inc.

Netscape Communications Corporation has not authorized, sponsored, or endorsed, or approved this publication and is not responsible for its content. Netscape and the Netscape Communications Corporate Logos, are trademarks and trade names of Netscape Communications Corporation. All other product names and/or logos are trademarks of their respective owners.

 Printed on recycled paper.

This book is dedicated to the future, particularly that of

Merissa Courtright, Abby Courtright,
Rebecca Perse, and Jonathan Perse

CONTENTS

CHAPTER 1

Why the Internet?
Why Human Communication?

As we approach the year 2000, no part of our existence has exhibited more frequent change than the technology surrounding electronic communication. One can hardly pick up a newspaper or listen to a news broadcast without learning of some new innovation, usually involving that global communication medium referred to as the Internet.

In response to this explosion of communication technology, this book is dedicated to the premise that students of human communication—regardless of their specific area of study—must master the use of electronics to function successfully as professionals in the next century. The alternative (and we do *not* believe this is too strong an assertion) is to condemn oneself to a level of technological illiteracy equivalent to not being able to read at the turn of the last century.

Accordingly, this book will provide the guidance, the vocabulary, and a set of skills necessary to launch communication students on their journey toward this technological competency. We must quickly add, however, that no book can hope to produce more than a preliminary understanding. Students must practice, explore, and experiment with these various communication tools if they are to attain the required level of mastery. From the students' perspective, the goal should be to feel as comfortable with these Internet technologies as they do when dialing a long-distance phone call or obtaining cash from the local ATM. This book will help, but it cannot serve as a substitute for direct experience.

WHAT IS THE INTERNET?

Whether used as part of a curse or a compliment, no computer term is bandied about with more all-encompassing frequency than the label *Internet*. This suggests that the best place to begin our journey is to demystify "the **Net**" by describing just exactly what knowledgeable people mean when they refer to the Internet.

1

Perhaps the easiest way to explore this term is to consider its two syllables separately. "Net" is an abbreviation for "network," which refers to any number of computers that are linked or connected and, thus, able to share information. In the early days of networking, there were several unconnected networks such as **BITNET** (for universities) or **MILNET** (for the military). The Internet, and thus the prefix "inter," arose when these several independent networks were joined through high-speed phone lines into a single worldwide network of computers.

The Internet and Your Computer

Although numerous features of the Internet make it useful and attractive, none is more important than the fact that it can be accessed and used through almost any type of computer, including types that are otherwise incompatible with each other. Hence, whether a student has access to a **PC**, a Macintosh (**Mac**), or even a terminal connected to his or her university's **mainframe**, electronic communication is possible via the Internet. These different machines and their operating systems are often called **platforms**, and they cannot communicate directly with each other. Try putting a Mac disk into a PC and see what happens. You won't harm the machine or the disk, but neither will you be able to use it.

The Internet, in contrast, is said to be platform independent, thus allowing communication back and forth over the network among any of these computers. Macs still cannot talk directly to PCs or mainframes (or vice versa), but over the Internet they share information as though they were exactly the same machine.

To remain true to this spirit of independence, the suggestions, directions, and assistance we provide in this book will also be platform independent. The authors both personally use PCs, and all of our illustrations and graphics are captured from the computers we use daily; however, we will make every effort to ensure that our advice and directions are equally applicable to all makes and models of computers. More importantly, where incompatibilities are unavoidable, we will say so explicitly.

WHAT IS THE INTERNET GOOD FOR?

There are no doubt numerous, acceptable ways to divide the various tasks one can perform on the Internet, but we have decided to segment these functions into two categories: (1) communicating and (2) accessing information. Each of these categories, of course, will contain several specific skills that communication students should strive to master. We will briefly describe these activities in this introductory section, while reserving a detailed discussion, including instructions for their use, for later chapters.

Communicating

One of the most obvious uses of the Internet for students of communication is actually communicating their thoughts and ideas to another individual. Such correspondence is both necessary and important. As we shall see, however, the Internet also allows communicating with numerous individuals simultaneously, as well as sending and receiving word-processed documents, data files, audio and video files, and even computer programs.

E-mail. Undoubtedly, the most frequent use of the Internet and, in fact, both large and small computer networks is individual correspondence by **electronic mail** (e-mail). Whether sending a quick "hello" to a distant friend, a request for assistance with an academic project, or even our opinion to our elected representatives, e-mail is rapidly becoming the medium of choice.

In Chapter 2 we will devote considerable space to discussing various facets of this important computer skill. One additional feature of e-mail that we will stress in that chapter is the ability to include **attachments** with one's e-mail. Simply stated, attachments are files that are included with or "attached" to the body of an e-mail message. As mentioned above, attachments can consist of additional text for consideration by the reader. More importantly, however, users of e-mail can also attach **binary files**, that is, files that contain computer codes (1s and 0s, hence the term "binary") rather than ordinary text.

Binary files might be created with a word processor and, thus, contain directions for sophisticated formatting, such as, boldface, italics, special margins, and so forth. As an example, the drafts of chapters of this book were attached to e-mail (in exactly the format you are reading) and sent between the two authors literally dozens of times.

Besides documents, a binary file might also be a spreadsheet, statistical output, a graph, a chart, or a picture. In fact, binary files attached to e-mail might even be actual programs that can run without alteration on the receiver's computer. If you have ever wanted to share your writing with someone else (say, your professor for some preliminary feedback), then you will find attachments such as these to be an invaluable tool.

Newsgroups. Every student beyond the grade of kindergarten is familiar with the concept of a bulletin board for posting words and pictures. Other than the family refrigerator, bulletin boards are perhaps the only place that most of us ever had our artwork displayed. This long familiarity should be comforting, because newsgroups are the equivalent of electronic bulletin boards.

Newsgroups are similar to e-mail, in that individuals who subscribe to the newsgroup can send or post messages and are able to reply to messages of others. Newsgroups are also similar to e-mail because you can include attachments to your postings; this allows subscribers to share all types of binary files.

Newsgroups are usually dedicated to a single topic (collecting antique fountain pens, using a new computer program, or discussions of the Bruce Springsteen fan club, to name a few) and can have many or few participants, depending on the general interest of the topic. A popular site may have thousands of messages posted each year.

The primary difference between newsgroups and e-mail is the audience. Newsgroups, like bulletin boards, have an audience that is much more public and, in some cases, largely anonymous. There certainly are exceptions (for example, a newsgroup dedicated solely to a communication class would be restricted to registered students), but posting messages to a newsgroup is often the electronic equivalent of posting an open note on a public bulletin board. Anyone who ventures by can read it.

Newsgroups differ from e-mail in another fundamental way: e-mail comes to the individual, but the individual must take action to go to a newsgroup. The analogy to bulletin boards still holds. Regular postal mail is delivered to your mailbox at home; you must travel to a public place to read the notes on a bulletin board.

For students of human communication, this difference raises an interesting distinction between active and passive communication media. E-mail comes to the individual and, therefore, falls closer to the passive end of the continuum (but not nearly as passive as television). Newsgroups, on the other hand, require purposeful behavior on the part of the subscriber (for example, to **log on** to the newsgroup) and are thus a more active medium. We will visit this comparison between active and passive media again. In the meantime, whether this makes a difference in how we use and respond to various electronic media would be an interesting question to raise with your classmates and instructor.

Listservs. To continue this active/passive comparison for a moment, listserv groups are like newsgroups in almost every respect, except that the postings are delivered to a subscriber's e-mail account. Similarly, to post a message to a listserv, a subscriber composes a regular e-mail message, but mails it to a central listserv address rather than to an individual. This makes listservs a type of electronic mass mailing.

Of course, the reverse is also true: a subscriber automatically receives each and every message that is sent to the central listserv address. Although the comparison to receiving "junk mail" is not quite fitting, being a member of an active listserv and receiving several dozen messages a day (only a few of which are of interest) will quickly bring that term to mind. For this reason, many people prefer newsgroups over the more passive listservs. People using newsgroups need to exert some effort to retrieve their messages, but they can do so at their convenience and they can ignore uninteresting postings.

FTP. The acronym **"FTP"** stands for **file transfer protocol**, which is the standard method of transferring entire files from one computer to another across the Internet. To be honest, "FTP-ing" only partially involves communicating with other individuals. Still, we think it is so important that we will mention this activity twice in this book.

To transfer files across the Internet, the two computers involved must accept a relationship: one must act as a **server** and the other must become a **client**. The server and the client can both send and receive files from each other, but the server is always in control of the transfer process.

The reason for this arrangement is, simply stated, security. The server computer can, and frequently does, require an individual to be recognized with a name and a password before transfers can take place. The client computer, on the other hand, must send that name and password for its attempts at transfer to be successful. The reason for this relationship is relatively obvious. Would you want everyone and anyone to have access to all of the files on your computer? Of course not. That is why this arrangement has been established. You can exchange files between, say, the computer in your apartment or dorm room and the university's mainframe, but no one else will have access to your files.

At a later, more prosperous, time in your life, you may wish to exchange files between the computer in your home study and the one in your office. Whether you make such exchanges often or infrequently, you will not want your personal and sometimes highly confidential files available to anyone who happens to stumble across your Internet address (including your professional competitors, who won't just *happen* to stumble across anything!). In these instances, you will appreciate the security provided by the client/server relationship.

Now that we have warned you sufficiently, we should also tell you that the use of FTP is a wonderful way to share information with friends and colleagues. This is why we classify this skill under the label of "communication." Assuming that your computers are networked, you can provide each person in your workgroup with a name and password on your computer, yet restrict them to a single directory or folder (such as, the "Our Project" folder). This gives them the freedom to read and write to selected files on your machine but, more importantly, gives *you* control over exactly which folders and files are available to them.

Shortly, we will suggest that a somewhat less controlled form of FTP-ing is an invaluable form of accessing information. As you will see, the difference is the amount and type of security involved. Sometimes, you may actually want anybody and everybody to have access to a file. That is an important need, but it is not what we are currently discussing. Communicating through the transfer of files assumes a selective and secure environment. In the hands of a competent user, FTP can provide precisely that type of relationship.

Real-time Communication. The several types of electronic communication we have discussed do not require the sender and receiver to be simultaneously online. This type of exchange is called **asynchronous** communication, indicating that the two or more individuals involved do not have to "synchronize" their computer usage. In contrast, talking to another on the telephone or engaging in a face-to-face interaction would be described as **synchronous** communication.

The Internet will support a form of synchronous communication, frequently referred to as "chatting." The formal name for this electronic medium is **Internet Relay Chat**. IRC is analogous to a CB radio, with numerous channels where individuals can join on-going chats about defined topics (for example, current events or sports). Users can also arrange to have a private conversation with one or more people. Unlike a radio, however, IRCs require users to type messages back and forth in a form of written conversation.

Recently, innovations have appeared that have the potential to make synchronous communication more useful and easier to conduct. For example, several companies have introduced an Internet version of a chalkboard, called a white board because of its white color. These boards let users share graphs, charts, pictures, and even handwritten messages in real time over the Internet. Although this development is interesting, it strikes us more as a useful addition to phone conversations than an independent form of communication. Technology is moving so fast, however, that in a few months we may have to admit that our opinion was totally wrongheaded.

While we are on the topic of phone calls, another very recent innovation is the use of the Internet to transmit real-time voice messages, thus approximating long- distance phone service without the long-distance charges (although buying a computer solely for this purpose would make for some pretty expensive conversations). The current quality of these conversations is only somewhat better than the childhood communication device of two tin cans connected by a string, so this technology won't be putting the phone company out of business any time soon.

We will not discuss these new trends in detail in the remainder of this book. Although the possibilities are fascinating, these technologies are still very much in their infancy, and any further description or commentary would be pure speculation. Moreover, the importance of these new trends for students of human communication remains unproven. Stay tuned, however, for today's unproven technologies could well be mainstream communication media in the near future.

Accessing Information

No feature of the Internet will be more helpful to students than the ability it affords to find massive amounts of information on an almost unlimited number of topics. In fact, some of the suggestions we will offer in later chapters will actually focus on how to obtain less (but better) information from the Internet. Whether you need the smallest of details (What time was *I Love Lucy* broadcast in 1955?) or background information about notable historical events (such as the bombing of Pearl Harbor), access to and knowledge of the Internet provides a distinct advantage.

Communication students, more particularly, can use the Internet to assist them in almost every course they take. Public speaking topics, FCC documents, history of television programs, or just basic reference materials can make preparation for classes much more efficient. Although the Internet is hardly prepared to replace a university's research-oriented library, students can frequently obtain the basic information they require, or at least acquire some focus and direction that will make their library searches more successful.

The World Wide Web. When the average person thinks of the Internet, chances are they are thinking of the **World Wide Web**, sometimes referred to by the initials **WWW**, but most often simply called the **Web**. When describing the Web, two terms immediately come to mind: **multimedia** and **hypertext**. The Web is certainly able to provide information in multiple forms or media, including text, pictures, audio, and (although less than perfect) even video. The potentially rich combination of these various media is, without doubt, what makes browsing the Web both interesting and so worthwhile as a source of information.

Equally important to the success of the Web is its use of hypertext or "linking." Creators of Web pages can make any word or phrase, or even parts of a picture, a direct link to any type or medium of information, whether it is located in another part of the same page or on a totally different page created by another individual or organization. By simply clicking the mouse on one of these links, the user is immediately—given the millions of users on the Internet, it's sometimes a bit slower than "immediately"—taken to that new source of information.

To illustrate this concept, we have captured the Web page for *The New York Times* and have displayed it in Figure 1.1. All of the sections, the underlined text, and even the main picture are direct links to other sections or to specific stories. *The Times* does not use audio or video clips in its pages, but if it did, the concept of clicking on a hyperlink to see or hear them would be the same.

Perhaps the easiest way to gain an elementary understanding of the Web is to borrow two terms from the theater, namely, backstage and front stage. Behind each and every page you view on the Web (the "backstage") is a sophisticated set of computer instructions referred to as **HyperText Markup Language** or **HTML.** The HTML controls the appearance of the Web page, and designates the text or pictures that will serve as hyperlinks. This computer language, however, operates completely behind the scenes and should not concern you. Unless you wish to create your own Web pages, you will neither encounter nor use HTML.

All parts of a Web page (text, pictures, audio files, etc.), as well as the HTML instructions for formatting them, reside on a host computer that is called a server. The function of a server is very much the same as we described during our discussion of FTP: it controls the interaction between itself and your computer.

As the viewer of Web pages, you are the "audience" that sits in front of the stage. Your ability to view, however, comes from the use of a Web **browser** that serves as a client to the server computer. When you click on a hyperlink, the browser issues a request to the server to send the desired information. The server, in response, delivers the information along with the HTML formatting instructions. These instructions are interpreted by the browser and placed on the computer screen in the form of a multimedia Web page.

The browser software, therefore, is what you must master to use the Web effectively. Throughout this book, we will focus our descriptions and explanations on the browser by Netscape Inc. The reason for this is that Netscape currently accounts for over 80% of all of the browsers in use. Other browsers certainly exist (for example, Internet Explorer from Microsoft), but are used by far fewer

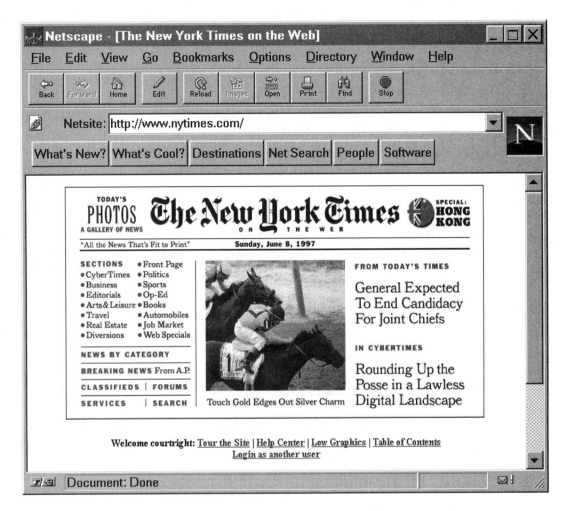

Figure 1.1 (Copyright © 1997 by The New York Times Co. Reprinted by permission. Copyright © 1996 Netscape Communications Corp. Used with permission. All Rights Reserved. This electronic file or page may not be reprinted or copied without the express written permission of Netscape.)

people. In any case, if you become knowledgeable about one browser, the effort required to learn another will be minimal.

With this in mind, we will spend a great deal of time describing how to use Netscape effectively in Chapter 3.

FTP. Earlier we described the use of file transfer protocol in the context of a secure environment—that is, to access files on another computer you must supply the proper log-on ID and a password. We suggested that this arrangement allowed two or more people working on the same project to share files, making corrections or changes as needed. Those without knowledge of the password, on the other hand, would be denied access.

In this section, we will introduce the transfer of files in an unsecured environment. In this context, the server does not require an ID or password. Rather, the server is open to anyone who wishes to transfer a file or a program to their own computer. Because no identification is required, this type of transfer is called **anonymous FTP**.

Anonymous FTP is widely used on the Internet as a way to share information in the form of **FAQ** files, that is, "frequently asked questions." Many hardware and software companies, for example, maintain anonymous FTP sites with FAQ files about their product. For example, if you are having a problem with your word processor or your monitor isn't displaying the correct colors, these files will often contain the right setting or a handy tip that will solve your problem.

Another use for anonymous FTP is to obtain actual working programs over the Internet. Both individuals and small companies write excellent software but don't have the marketing capability of an IBM or a Microsoft. Instead, they market their programs as **shareware**, or "try and then buy," by placing them on the Internet for downloading via FTP. This approach relies totally on the honor system; if you use the program beyond the trial period, you are expected to pay for it. Similarly, even the largest companies offer upgrades or fixes to existing programs, and they will make these available exclusively through anonymous FTP.

The more time you spend using your computer to explore the Internet, the more you will come to appreciate the power and utility of this method of acquiring information and software. We will explore various approaches to FTP-ing in Chapter 5. If you become serious about the Internet, that chapter will be one of the most important in this book.

In Brief: Telnet and Gopher. The two technologies called **telnet** and **gopher** have been available for quite a few years. They are the predecessors of Web browsers and, more recently, visually-oriented FTP clients. For that reason they are widely available, and for some students with text-based access to the Internet, they are the *only* tools available. For reasons that we will explain shortly, we will not discuss these tools in later chapters, choosing instead to provide only a brief description in this introductory chapter.

Using a telnet client is the most basic and fundamental way to access information on another computer. Telnet, simply described, is the Internet's version of the computer terminal. The client/server relationship guides a telnet session in a secured environment, thus requiring an ID and password to log on. When connected, however, instead of the visually rich window of a Web browser, the user is faced with a text-only connection in which instructions (for example, copy, delete, print) must be typed in at a **command line**. When used from a Windows-based PC or a Mac, some telnet clients have limited support for mouse clicks, but the actual work on the host computer is always done by typing on the command line.

Similarly, telnet sessions usually allow users to read and change their files by using a text-based editor. If you have worked only in Windows or on a Mac, you will find these editors much different and most likely quite unsatisfactory. As we said before, they are textually based and do not support any type of mouse movement. Thus, you must move through a file using the cursor keys or by typing commands such as "top," "bottom," "down 10," and so forth. Sometimes the necessary keystrokes are even more abstract, such as using "ctrl-v" (holding down the control key and typing "v") to move down a single page. You can surely edit a file this way, but to quote the late Dr. Seuss, "you will not like it, not one little bit."

Figure 1.2 (p. 12) illustrates a telnet session in which the text from the previous paragraph is being edited using a text editor. At the bottom of the screen are keystrokes (the ^ symbolizes the control key) that are used as shortcuts for various commands. The black "box" in the middle of the screen is the cursor.

Make no mistake, telnet is a relatively old technology and, for that reason, many people would rather not use it. Be that as it may, at many universities, if you do not have your own computer in your dorm or apartment, you may be forced to use a university terminal where telnet is the most likely medium of communication. You may not like it, but you'll most likely have to learn it.

Gopher clients are also textually based, but they operate in an unsecured environment, much in the spirit of anonymous FTP. Before the widespread use of Web browsers, the only way to locate and obtain information from the Internet was through gopher. Like Netscape, a gopher client is a type of browser that presents information in the form of a menu. The menu items, in turn, are hyperlinks that take you either to another more specific menu or directly to the information you desire. Recall, however, that the information is almost always provided in the form of text.

A basic gopher menu (accessed through a telnet session) is displayed in Figure 1.3 (p. 13). If a user wanted information about upcoming activities on

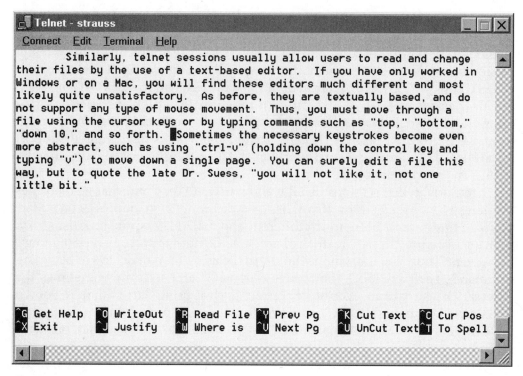

Figure 1.2

campus, he or she would use the cursor to move down to item 5 and then press the Enter key. Another menu would then appear, and the process would begin again. Finally, the user would arrive at the desired information, which would be displayed in the form of a text file.

As we stated earlier, we will not discuss these two technologies in detail in this book. In terms of telnet, there are so many different telnet clients (quite a few of these are free via FTP), that we could not begin to cover them all. More importantly, the knowledge necessary to use telnet effectively is actually the set of commands for the host computer, usually UNIX commands. Using UNIX effectively is an important skill but not one that is an appropriate topic for this book.

Our reason for ignoring gopher is that all of the functions of this information technology have been incorporated into the latest Web browsers. Netscape, for example, can access information from any gopher server, thus making the mastery

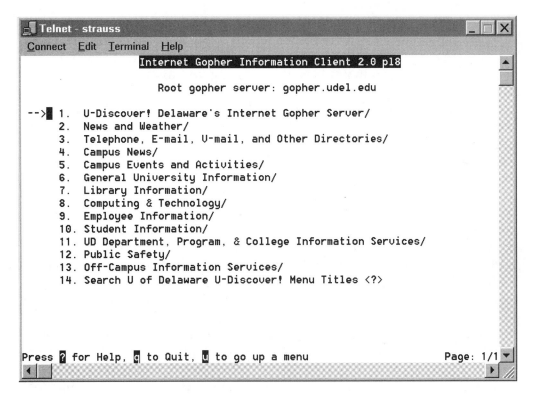

Figure 1.3

of a gopher client unnecessary. More importantly, because Web browsers are visually (as opposed to textually) oriented and make complete use of the mouse, you will find them much easier and much more pleasant to use. There is plenty of information to be found at gopher sites, but that information can be located and displayed just like any other type of information on the Web.

VIRUSES

Any guide to the Internet should include a discussion of viruses, the online "disease." The biological analogy is a good one. A **virus** is a computer program that sends copies of itself to "infect" other programs. Viruses are parasites. They cannot exist independently, but instead must reside in other programs. Viruses act on their own; once they are attached to computer programs, they replicate and infect independently.

Most viruses are the results of childish technological pranks. They can be annoying (by slowing down the host computer's speed or by flashing messages), but most are harmless. A small percentage of viruses, however, are deadly. They can overwrite (and eliminate) files, thus causing you to lose the data on your floppy or hard disks.

Viruses have also been the topic of many of the hoaxes on the Internet. Most of you have probably heard about (or even received e-mail about) the "Good Times" virus. Rumors about this virus have been circulating since 1994. The best way to protect yourself from being fooled by hoaxes and to protect your files from real viruses is to understand how viruses are spread.

Viruses are parasites of programs. They reside silently in a computer program until that program is run. As a result, viruses can only be spread in computer programs or macros (codes of instructions to the computer). Viruses are not spread in data files, such as word-processing documents, e-mail, or multimedia files. You cannot get a virus by reading e-mail or other documents, reading Web pages, or even simply by downloading files. The only way to get a virus is to run the program in which it resides. Running an infected computer program stimulates the virus to replicate and spread.

Unfortunately, there are several ways that students can encounter infected computer programs, especially when they use computer labs. Although they are becoming less common, it is still possible to become infected with **boot sector viruses**. Boot sector viruses reside in the boot, or system start-up, program. Boot sector viruses can be passed from infected hard drives in computer labs to students' own floppy disks. Boot sector viruses may be harmless, but some can wipe out important files and prevent computers from being able to boot, or start up.

Macro viruses are still fairly new, but are becoming more common. Macro viruses affect the macro (or template) parts of programs. Macros are not seen directly by most users, but every time you create a document with your word-processing program, you use a macro or template (usually the "new document" template). A macro virus spreads when the macro is turned on and can either corrupt the file or make it impossible to save the file.

Students who are facile with the Internet may also **download** programs infected with viruses. Remember that viruses are spread by running programs, not simply by downloading them. However, if programs with viruses are run without checking for viruses, the virus will infect the host computer.

There are some simple steps you can take to protect your computer, disks, and files from viruses. First, get some anti-virus software. This type of software detects and disinfects computer viruses. Some anti-virus software is available as shareware; some schools have site licenses for their staff and students. Perhaps the most important part of this recommendation is that you use the software and update it regularly. If you use computer labs, ask the staff to check your disks for viruses before and after using the lab's computers. Also use the software to check out any files that you download.

Second, avoid sharing disks with others. If you must use someone else's disks, use anti-virus software to check them out first. If you must put your disks in someone else's computer, flip the "write-protect" tab on your disk, so no files can be inadvertently copied onto your disk. Practice safe computing.

Third, look (and think!) before you download. Use reputable sites for downloading shareware. Avoid downloading "underground" software that allows you to cheat (to use a commercial Internet site without paying their charges). Finally, use your anti-virus software to check any files you download before you run them.

Fourth, back up everything. Back up your work, your programs, your files, and your disks. Back up regularly and often. Store your backups in a safe place. Thus, if a virus should infect your work, you will still be able to restore your computer and its files back to good health.

ESTABLISHING YOUR INTERNET ACCOUNT

There are basically only three ways for university students to gain access to the Internet. You must establish an Internet account (1) with your university, (2) with a commercial service (America On-Line, CompuServe, or Prodigy, for example), or (3) with an Internet service provider. This latter group consists of commercial services, and these are best located by looking in the yellow pages of your phone directory. Most students will choose to establish an account with their university because this service is provided as part of your registration and, perhaps more importantly, it is paid for by a portion of your tuition.

Every university, of course, has a slightly different process for establishing an active account. If you do not have a computer account already, you will need to check with the computing folks on your campus. They will ask you to provide some basic information and, in return, will issue you a log-on ID and a preliminary password. **Make certain you quickly change that password!** Use a word, a name, or a series of letters that you can remember but that cannot be easily guessed by others. Your birthday or your middle name are too obvious, but the street where your cousin lives or your grandmother's maiden name are pretty safe bets.

Once you are satisfied that you have a reasonably safe password, **do not reveal it to anyone!** For example, the two authors of this book have worked closely over many years, yet they do not know each other's passwords, and would not think to ask. Similarly, be very careful when typing your password that others are not watching with the intent to copy it. Your password is the key to keeping your files and your information secure. Giving it to someone else is the equivalent of inviting them to browse through your private material. Right now you may not have much information on your computer that is worth safeguarding, but someday you will. Now is not too soon to practice the necessary security.

AN EMPHASIS ON ETHICS

Successful computing in general, and the use of the Internet in particular, require a degree of cooperation and civility unlike that needed in many other endeavors. Frequently, the actions you take or the commands you issue can have a major impact (mostly a negative impact) on other computer users. In contrast, some thoughtfulness coupled with just a bit of concern about others can make everyone's life on the Internet more productive and more enjoyable.

We will discuss this thoughtfulness and concern under the label computer ethics. We will not carry on an extended, philosophical discussion of what it means to be "ethical." For our purposes, we will define ethics simply as "doing the right thing, even when no one is looking" and equally important, "behaving properly, even when there is no chance of being caught." If every Internet user followed these simple rules, there would be no need for the security and safeguards we will discuss in this book. But alas . . . you will almost certainly encounter users who are up to no good. Hence, although we implore you to be ethical, we will also help you to protect yourself against those who are not.

To share our thoughts about what it means to "do right" and "behave properly," we will end each chapter of this book with a short section on computer ethics. We promise we will not preach, nor will we offer a series of "thou shalt nots." We do, however, believe that it is our responsibility to make certain you are aware of what behavior is appropriate and what is considered unacceptable. We truly hope you will choose to be ethical, because we are also Internet users and your behavior affects us along with everybody else.

CHAPTER 2

Electronic Mail

Using electronic mail to communicate person-to-person is not only the oldest use of the Internet, but it is also the most common use. In 1997, for example, 15% of the U.S. population used e-mail, and within five years that number should rise to 50% (*Educom Review*, March/April, 1997, p. 8). Electronic mail works like regular mail (computer users often call it "snail mail"), but once you are comfortable using e-mail, you will see that it has many advantages over traditional mail.

- E-mail messages are delivered quickly, almost instantaneously, to users on the same computer systems and usually in less than a day, no matter how far the mail has to travel.
- E-mail is convenient to use. You don't have to worry about sending e-mail only when you know that the person you want to reach is near a computer. The message will wait in their **in-box** until the person is ready to read their mail. And you can deal with your own e-mail messages at your convenience, for example, between classes, late at night, or early in the morning.
- E-mail is an economical way to correspond with others. The cost of sending e-mail is usually unrelated to the distance it must travel or the length of the message.
- E-mail is an informal medium. Although you should always be careful about spelling, grammar, and punctuation in anything that you write, e-mail is designed for concise and efficient communication. Because the **header** indicates who the message is from and the date of delivery and because your mail program can automatically add your **signature** to your message, you don't need to follow the formal structure of typical letters. Thus, e-mail is perfect for quick notes!
- E-mail can be used to send all sorts of information. Most mail programs make it easy to **attach** graphics, multimedia (sound and video) files, formatted documents, Web pages, and software.

Warning!

E-mail is missing an important communication channel: the nonverbal. Because e-mail is a printed medium, readers cannot hear the tone of your voice or see your facial expressions. So, it is difficult to signal emotions in your e-mail. Be careful about including humor or sarcasm because it can be misinterpreted. Some e-mail users use **emoticons** to signal some simple emotions like happiness and sadness.

EMOTICON	MEANING
:)	I'm happy
:(	I'm sad
:-)	I'm happy (with a nose)
:-(	I'm sad (with a nose)
:-D	I'm laughing
;-)	I'm winking

Figure 2.1

UNDERSTANDING E-MAIL ADDRESSES

Domain Name System

Just as there is a standard format for addressing envelopes for the U.S. mail (recipient's name, street address, city, state, and zip code), there is a standard format for e-mail addresses. The Internet first used only numbers for addresses. These **Internet Protocol** (or **IP**) addresses are still used to indicate a specific computer within a network (the IP address for the second author's computer, which is part of the University of Delaware network, is 128.175.30.73). Now IP addresses are rarely used by nontechnical users. Instead, most of us use addresses that follow the **Domain Name System** (or **DNS**), which substitutes for IP numbers.

In this system, every e-mail address is made up of the user's log-on name or user ID (something that personally identifies you on the computer system), the @ (or "at") sign, and the domain name (including any subdomains). The domain and subdomain names are separated by periods (pronounced "dot") and take the place of the IP address. The exact form of any e-mail address will depend on the system that the organization uses. Here is the e-mail address of the first author of this book:

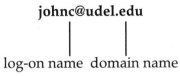

This is a rather simple address that includes only a log-on name and a domain name. Other e-mail addresses include subdomain names as well. The address to contact Newt Gingrich, the speaker of the House of Representatives, is:

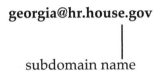

You can tell what kind of organization the domain is by the letters at the end of the address. If you have an Internet account with your university, your address will end with .edu, which is used for all U.S. educational institutions. Speaker Gingrich's address ends in .gov, which is used for all government organizations. Addresses with commercial accounts end in .com (such as aol.com) and nonprofit organizations use .org. Other domain names are .int (international organizations), .mil (U.S. military), and .net (network resources).

Because the Internet is growing so quickly, at the beginning of 1997 there was some discussion about adding seven new domain names: .arts (cultural and entertainment organizations), .firm (businesses), .info (information services), .nom (individuals), .rec (recreation/entertainment), .store (businesses offering goods for sale), and .web (organizations with Web-related activities). No doubt we will see those domain names in use soon.

Mail sent outside the United States should also include a two-letter country code. There are too many to list here (as many as there are countries in the world). Some relatively obvious examples of those codes are .ca (Canada), .uk (United Kingdom), .il (Israel), .ng (Nigeria), .ec (Ecuador), and .tw (Taiwan). If you wanted to reach Daniel Chandler at the University of Wales, who is the **Webmaster** of the Media and Communication Studies Internet site, his address would include the country code for the United Kingdom:

dgc@aber.ac.uk

Finding E-mail Addresses

The easiest source of someone's e-mail address is the person with whom you wish to communicate. Most people now include their e-mail address on their correspondence as commonly as they include their phone numbers. Ask your friends and professors to give you their e-mail addresses so you can reach them whenever you want. If someone has sent you e-mail, their e-mail address will be in the message's header. Below in Figure 2.2 is an example of an e-mail header. We will talk more about headers later in this chapter.

Return-Path: eperse@UDel.edu
X-Sender: eperse@UDel.edu
Date: Fri, 21 Feb 1997 11:43:19 -0500
To: johnc@UDel.Edu
From: "Elizabeth M. Perse" <eperse@UDel.Edu>
Subject: Chapter 2

Figure 2.2

Another way to find someone's address is to use the **finger** command. Finger is a command for **Unix** computers that gives information about a user on that system. To find the e-mail address for someone on your own system, simply log onto your computer system and type:

finger *"name"* | more

Make certain you substitute the log-on ID of the person you wish to find for the word "name" (do not include the quote marks). The " | more" at the end is also a Unix command that displays the response one screen at a time. You move forward by hitting the space bar. The "more" suffix comes in handy if you have a common name such as Smith. Try it without the " | more" just once and you'll see what we mean.

The response to the finger command should be almost instantaneous and should resemble Figure 2.3.

You can also use the finger command to find people on other computer systems. This is no more difficult than including the @ followed by the domain name. For example, to find the second author's e-mail address, type:

finger perse@udel.edu

```
strauss~3:38pm>finger perse|more
Login name: eperse                    In real life: Elizabeth Perse
Directory: /home/strauss/usrc/4e/20160  Shell: /bin/tcsh
On since Mar 10 15:38:40 on pts/243 from eperse.comm.udel.edu
No unread mail
No Plan.
```

Figure 2.3

There are also many ways to find e-mail addresses from various directories on the Internet. Figure 1.3 (p. 12) in Chapter 1 showed the University of Delaware's gopher menu. Note that there are two menu items that could be sources for e-mail addresses: item 3 (telephone, e-mail, and other directories for on-campus e-mail addresses) and item 13, off-campus information services. So you could begin a search from your own school's gopher site.

Along these same lines, in Chapter 3 we will discuss how to use a browser to find information on the WWW. Almost every university that maintains a Web site has a hyperlink to names, phone numbers, and e-mail addresses of both faculty and students. Try looking for your friends who are attending other universities. Chances are that you'll have no trouble finding them.

Of course, not everyone you might wish to e-mail attends a university. For these individuals, there are several sites on the Web that use forms to enter the relevant information (for example, name, address, employer, etc.). This information is used to search for that particular person. To illustrate how simple it is to search for e-mail addresses in this manner, Figure 2.4 (p. 23) displays a screen capture a site for the Four11 directory.

Four11 is one of several Web site e-mail directories. As you can see, you simply type in the log-on ID and domain name (if you know it) of the person you are trying to locate, click on the "Search" button, and Four11 will return all of the matches it finds in its database.

Because new information sources find their way to the Web daily, we have not included a directory of those sites in this chapter. Instead, we've included a more comprehensive list of addresses for these resources in the Appendix to this book. In the jargon of the Web, these addresses are called **Uniform Resource**

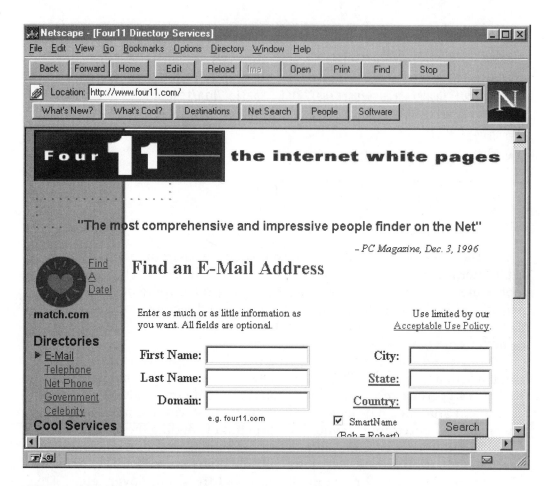

Figure 2.4 (Reproduced with the permission of Four11 Corporation.)

Locators (**URL**s) and will be discussed in detail in Chapter 3.

Our advice is to be creative when you're looking for an e-mail address. The Internet provides many routes to the same destination. A short while ago, one of us was looking for the e-mail address of a friend of one of our children who had moved away. We knew her name and the university she was attending. So, we went to her university's home page, found the link to the student directory, and then found her name, user ID, and e-mail address. The whole process took less than five minutes.

Keeping an Address Book

Once you've found the e-mail addresses of people with whom you wish to correspond, use your mail program to store them. Most mail programs have an **address book** feature to store and organize addresses. Some mail programs have a command to "save/take address" directly from an e-mail message you have received and write it to the address book. Some programs automatically add the address of any reply you make to the address book. For other programs, you may want to use the Windows "copy" and "paste" edit features to copy the e-mail addresses to your address book. And, of course, you can always opt for the old-fashioned way and choose to type those addresses in the address book yourself.

Another advantage of address books is that they can save time and key strokes. Most mail programs include address books that not only store addresses, but also allow you to use **nicknames**, or user-defined "shortcuts" for addresses. If your mail program has a nicknames feature, you will able to assign an easy-to-remember nickname for everyone in your address book. For example, when the authors e-mail each other, we type "john" or "betsy" in the header instead of the complete e-mail address. Our program recognizes those nicknames and inserts the longer address.

WAYS TO SEND E-MAIL

You can choose among many programs to use for e-mail. What program you use will depend on your Internet account. Not surprisingly, most students use the software provided by their school's computer system. Programs like Pine, Mail, and Elm are perfectly serviceable e-mail systems on many university computers.

Note that we didn't describe these programs as "outstanding" or "excellent." On the contrary, programs such as these will almost certainly seem difficult to use for students who are used to the graphical nature of Windows or a Macintosh, primarily because these older programs have no mouse support. As a result, users must move around the screen by using the cursor keys, compose messages by using awkward text-based editing, and issue commands by pressing keys, often two at a time, such as <control x> (the command for sending mail in Pine).

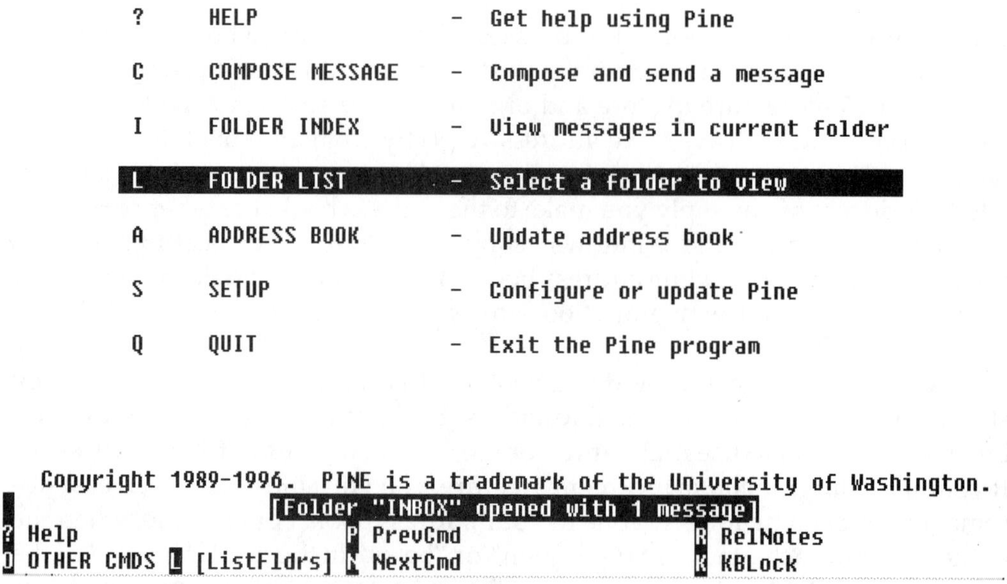

```
?       HELP                -   Get help using Pine

C       COMPOSE MESSAGE     -   Compose and send a message

I       FOLDER INDEX        -   View messages in current folder

L       FOLDER LIST         -   Select a folder to view

A       ADDRESS BOOK        -   Update address book

S       SETUP               -   Configure or update Pine

Q       QUIT                -   Exit the Pine program




Copyright 1989-1996.  PINE is a trademark of the University of Washington.
                [Folder "INBOX" opened with 1 message]
? Help                    P PrevCmd                      R RelNotes
O OTHER CMDS L [ListFldrs] N NextCmd                     K KBLock
```

Figure 2.5

Similarly, attaching and retrieving nontext files in these programs also requires several complicated and cumbersome steps. These programs have several advantages, however. They cost nothing to use, technical support is easy to find on campus, and these venerable old programs are very efficient despite their clumsiness. Figure 2.5 shows an example taken from Pine Mail.

If you have access to a computer connected directly to the Internet—either through your university system, a commercial provider, or an Internet service—you have several other options which are easier to use. Web browsers, such as Netscape and Internet Explorer, have all the features of other mail programs built right into the program. (The mail program from Netscape is displayed in Figure 2.6.) Once you configure the program, usually in an Options window, you can then create, send, and read messages easily.

The mail programs that are the easiest to use are those designed to operate directly on a personal computer. Both authors of this book use Eudora, a program that logs onto the university's mail system, retrieves our mail regularly, alerts us with a few seconds of music when we receive new mail, and stores out mail in various mailboxes, or folders, on our PCs (see Figure 2.7, p. 26). As a result, we

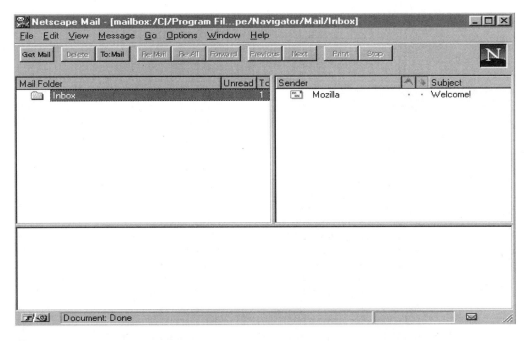

Figure 2.6 Copyright © 1996 Netscape Communications Corp. Used with permission. All rights reserved. This electronic file or page may not be reprinted or copied without the express written permission of Netscape.)

can read and send mail using all of the features of our PCs and, most importantly, avoid the antiquated text-based system on our university's mainframe.

The program we use is similar to many other competing programs on the market and it has many useful features, including a spelling checker, filters to send junk mail directly to the trash, "drag and drop" (using the mouse to move messages), and a direct link to the Netscape browser on our PCs so that with one "click" we can launch Netscape and go directly to any Web site whose URL is mentioned in our mail. Several other programs like Eudora are available as shareware that you can download using FTP.

THE BASICS OF E-MAIL

No matter which of the many available programs you use for your e-mail, the steps you take will be quite similar. Specific commands for each program differ, but the processes are essentially the same. Once you have practiced, you will

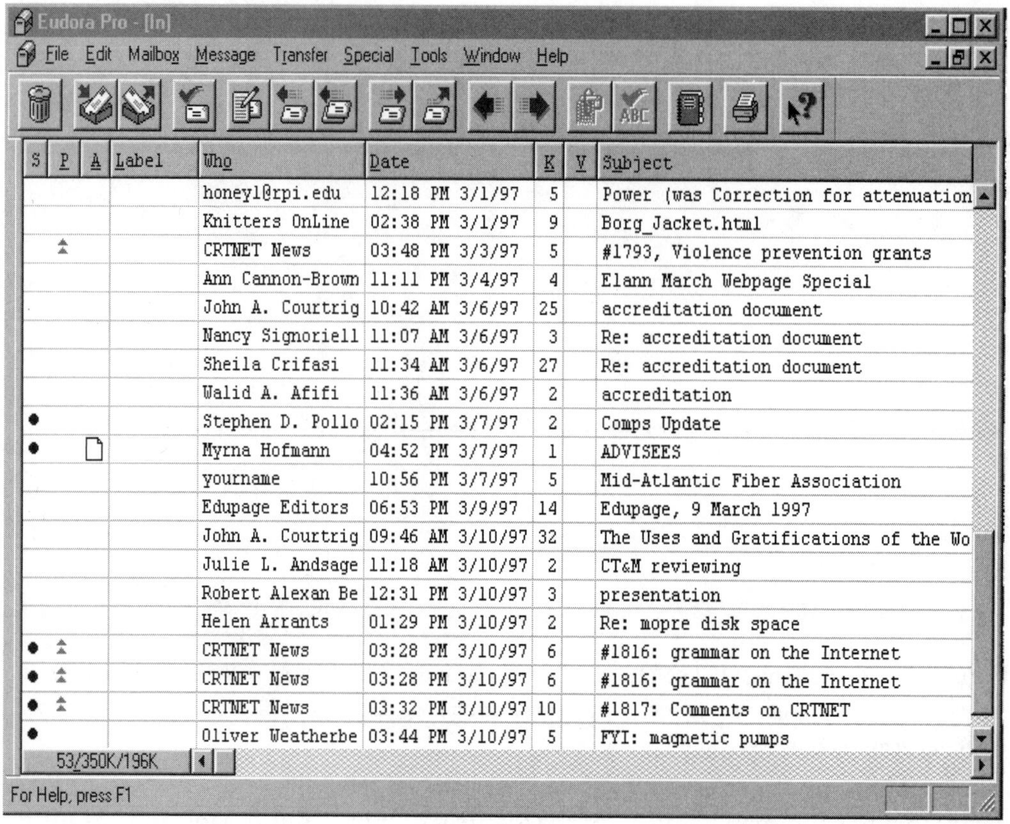

Figure 2.7

find e-mail etiquette quite simple. On **mainframe** computers, the commands are summarized at the bottom of the e-mail screen. On Windows and Mac systems, click on the Help menu to obtain assistance.

Sending

Sending e-mail messages is easy. Use the "compose," "new message," or whatever command the program recognizes to create a new e-mail message. With most programs, you will be presented with a blank header. Fill in the lines on the header. Type in the e-mail address (or nickname) of the recipient next to the word "To." The program will automatically insert your address next to "From."

Complete the "Subject" line to give your recipient some information about the message. You may also send the message to others by listing their addresses or nicknames next to "cc:" (carbon copy). Some programs have a blind carbon copy option that allows you to send copies without the primary recipient knowing this.

If you want to send the same message to several people, list the e-mail address (or nickname) for each person on a different line or separated by the punctuation dictated by the program. (Both Pine and Eudora use commas.) Or you can list additional respondents on the cc line in the header.

> **Tip:** Computers are unforgiving. Make sure that you type every part of the address correctly when sending e-mail. Even an unwanted space will keep your message from reaching its destination.

Then simply enter your message in the text area. If you are using a mainframe computer, you will probably use a rather unsophisticated text editor without many features. If your mail program is on a PC, you may be able to use "cut" and "paste" and a variety of other typical word processing-features, including spelling checkers.

> **Tip:** Use your computer's text editor (not word processor!) to create a signature file for your e-mail. A signature file includes a few lines of personal information that is automatically included at the end of every message that you send. We recommend that your signature include your name, snail mail address, phone and fax numbers. That way, your message is clearly identified and the respondent can contact you easily. Signatures become elaborate when they include quotations, poetry, or even stylized images. Don't become too "cutesy" with your signature. Embellishments can obscure important information, and large signatures waste disk space.

Although the most common use of e-mail is to exchange simple text messages, e-mail messages can include more complex information in attached files. Attachments can be simple text, but they can also be files with sophisticated formatting created by word processors, spreadsheets, and databases. Attachments have the advantage of being transferred as binary files (files that contain computer codes) so the format of documents is preserved, and files can be viewed and used by other programs on other computers. The authors of this book frequently attach document files to our e-mail and occasionally attach multimedia (audio and video) files. One advantage to using an Internet browser's mail program is that you can attach fully formatted Web pages to share with your correspondents. Be careful, though: e-mail with attachments is usually delivered as quickly as simple text messages, but large attachments take much longer. If the attachments are too large, they may be undeliverable.

Attaching files in PC-based mail programs is easy. Simply click on the "attach file" feature (usually in the Message menu), and type in the name of the file (including all the directory / folder information). Or you can use the browse feature to locate the file on your hard or floppy drive.

On mainframe computers, attaching files is a more complex process. First, you may have to FTP the file from your own computer or floppy disk to your mainframe computer account. Then, you will need to convert the file to a binary format. In Unix systems, for example, use the **uuencode** command. Then, attach the file. This process sounds more complicated than it really is, and many users who rely on mainframe e-mail systems don't use attachments for that reason. Check with your university's User Services Department about using uuencode. Perhaps they have installed some changes to make the handling of attachments easier.

Once you have completed the header, edited the text of the message, and attached any files, simply execute the Send command, or click on the Send button.

You have no control over when people read your e-mail, but you can be fairly sure that your message was received by the mail server unless it is bounced back to you. If mail is returned to you as "undeliverable," most mail servers include a message summarizing the problem. Look over that message. Most mail delivery problems are typing or spelling errors in the address. If that is the case, correct your error and resend the message. If the message is returned because the address is no longer valid on that domain, you should search for a new e-mail address.

Tip: Using nicknames and an address book will reduce the chances of sending undeliverable mail to people that you contact regularly.

Reading

Once you have started to use e-mail, it is wise to schedule a regular time to check and read your e-mail. Mainframe computers and commercial Internet providers usually tell you if you have new mail when you log on. The authors of this book keep our e-mail programs running constantly, so we know immediately when we have received mail.

To read your mail, start the mail program on the computer. Some programs may automatically list new messages; other programs will require you to go to the in-box. You will then see a directory, or list, of messages. The list will include the e-mail address of the person who sent you mail (or the nickname, if you have given that address a nickname) and the subject of the message provided by the sender. Figure 2.7 (p. 26) is an example of an in-box in Eudora. You can use that directory to filter your messages, if you wish. You can delete before reading any messages that you know are a waste of your time (for example, junk mail).

Once you have opened your in-box, reading mail is easy. Simply place the cursor on the message line in the in-box and press Enter (on most mainframe mail programs). On PC-based programs, double click on the message line. In both cases, the text of the message will appear on the screen.

Look for a line in the header notifying you that the message has an attachment. Follow your mail program's conventions for reading or using the attachment. With PC-based mail systems, you simply click on the attachment name or icon. The mail program will activate the appropriate application to allow you to read, use, or listen to the file. You may also save the file on your computer for future use.

Mail systems on mainframe computers, again, require more steps to read attachments. First, you may have to "extract" the file from the mail message. Then, if the file has been converted to a binary format, run the decoding program on your system (for example, **uudecode**). You may be able to read the file, but more likely you will want to FTP it to your PC to be read by the appropriate program.

Once you have read your e-mail, you have several possible options about how to respond. One, all-too-frequently overlooked response is to do nothing. This is an especially appropriate reaction when the message contains basic information and no response is required. Initially, it may seem polite to write back with a "Thanks" or "I got it," but you will soon realize that such messages require unnecessary time and attention from the person on the other end. Most e-mail correspondents will be happier if you simply read the information and forego the polite response.

Of course, some action is often necessary. Below we discuss four possible responses to e-mail.

Replying

One feature that you will use, no matter which mail program you have, is the Reply function. Replying is the easiest way to send mail back to someone who has sent you mail. Once you execute the Reply command or click on the Reply button, the program automatically creates a new message with a completed header. The header includes your address, the address of the person to whom you are responding, and the subject, which will be the same as in the original message.

Warning! You may want to reply to a message that has been sent to a mailing list or to many people at the same time. If you want to respond only to the source of the message, make sure that you don't send your reply to everyone on the list. Sending a "mass reply" not only confuses the unintended recipients and wastes their time, but also makes you look foolish or incompetent.

Most programs also give you the option of including the text of the message to which you are replying. This can be a good way to remind recipients of the context of their correspondence, especially if they do not have a copy of their message to you. The earlier message will be inserted in the mail and each line of the message will be preceded by a double arrow ">>". But, you should resist the temptation to always include the entire message; edit the message to include only the parts that are relevant to your reply.

Tip: Remember that if you receive a message with these double arrows in front of some of the text, that text has been forwarded from someone else.

Once you have edited the text of the message, simply execute the Send command, or click on the Send button.

Forwarding

You may often want to share the information in an e-mail message with others. The easiest way to do this is to forward the mail. In most programs, forwarding is a simple command. When you execute the Forward command, or click on the Forward button, the program will prompt you to fill in the forwarding addresses. Again, you can type the address, use a nickname from your address book, or even forward a message to an entire mailing list. The entire message, including the old header, is now ready to be forwarded. Remember that you don't have to forward the entire message. You may want to edit it before you send it to remove information that you don't want to share with others, to make the message easier to read by the recipients, and to save Internet resources.

The two authors of this book have received forwarded mail (unedited) so many times that the old headers filled screens and screens (not to mention disk space). Scrolling through all that is a waste of time. Be considerate when forwarding messages.

Once you have filled in the header and edited the message text, simply execute the Send command, or click on the Send button.

Saving

Most often you will want to delete a message after you've read and responded to it. Of course, you may receive information via e-mail that you need to save. For example, you might want to save messages about the topic of a paper until you are ready to begin to research and write your paper. Later in this chapter we will encourage you to be selective about what you save in order to conserve disk space and computer resources.

Most e-mail programs include some kind of filing system to organize your e-mail. The system may use **folders** or **mailboxes** to store messages. Whichever program you use, the filing system will display messages in various folders just as you see messages in the in-box, which is itself another folder. So, if you open a folder, you will see each message listed by sender and topic.

The most common folder is the **out-box** (sometime called the "sent mail" file). This folder holds copies of each message that you send. This is the only folder that does not list each message by sender (since all messages were sent by the same person). Instead, it lists the messages by the intended recipient. The out-box is a good way to record your own messages, but it can easily become overfilled and disorganized.

Folders can be an efficient way to store and organize e-mail messages. We believe that the best way to store messages is to create a set of folders, one for each meaningful topic. Then, save relevant e-mail in those folders. For example, you might be planning a class presentation about the accuracy of television news coverage of the bombing of the Oklahoma City Federal Building. As part of your research, you have e-mailed friends who live in Oklahoma City. When you get their responses, you will find it helpful to make a new folder, called "Bombing," and store those messages in that folder.

You might also have a class in which the teacher communicates to the class regularly via e-mail. The teacher might send copies of old tests, class lists, or study hints. For that semester, you might find it helpful to have a folder named for that class, to store those messages.

> **Tip:** Don't use your in-box as a "things to do" list. Instead, make a "to-do" folder and transfer messages that you need to act on into that folder. Keep your in-box clean so you won't lose new or important messages.
>
> **Another tip:** Don't make too many folders. If your filing system is too complex, you will forget where you have filed your messages. Keep your system simple!

Printing

You won't need to print every message, but sometimes you will want a hard copy of the message. The authors of this book once sent copies of a class list (with names, phone numbers, and e-mail addresses) to students enrolled in their class. We expect that most of the students printed this list to keep for reference in their course notebooks. To print, simply execute the Print command. The Pine program, a mainframe mail program, uses the command "Y." For Windows and Mac programs, simply click on the Print button.

Saving Disk Space

No matter which mail program you use, you will have limited resources for e-mail. Mainframe computer systems allocate only a specific amount of disk storage space for each user. Once you discover how easy and convenient e-mail is, you will quickly fill up that space, if you aren't careful. Even if you are sending and receiving e-mail on your PC, storing messages will use up hard disk storage. Although newer computers come equipped with large hard drives, it's still good practice to clean out your folders periodically to free up disk space.

Most e-mail programs keep a copy of each message that you send in an out-box. This is a useful feature that allows you to refer to old correspondence, but if you send lots of e-mail, the out-box will quickly consume a good deal of disk space. Once a month, take time to go over the messages in your out-box. Delete all messages that you don't need. If a message is particularly important, you might want to transfer it to another folder related to the topic of the message.

Each semester you should look over your entire mail filing system. Delete outdated messages and folders. Once you've made your presentation on the

Oklahoma City bombing, for example, you can delete those messages along with the entire folder.

An e-mail filing system is just like any other filing system. It will break down if it isn't well maintained. Clean it up regularly.

THE ETHICS OF COMMUNICATING WITH E-MAIL

- Remember the purpose of e-mail is to communicate. Make your messages short, to the point, and easy to read. Always include information that makes it easy for the recipient to get in touch with you.
- Don't use special characters (such as italics and underlining) because they may appear as gibberish on some computer systems. If you MUST use emphasis you can type important words in capital letters or else type a single underscore character before and after the word (_emphasis_).
- Don't SHOUT! Using all capital letters makes your messages difficult to read and your reader may take offense.
- Check for messages and respond to your e-mail regularly. Be courteous and treat e-mail as you would treat your answering machine messages.
- E-mail does not have the privacy or security of regular mail. Not only can messages be read by others, but they can also be forwarded to other users. Be discreet. Ask yourself: Would I be embarrassed or ashamed if I read my words in tomorrow's newspaper? If you answer "yes," then don't send that message.
- You should never intentionally harass someone. Also be careful to avoid unintentional harassment with e-mail. Remember that your name and e-mail address are included in the header, so if you're nasty, you're likely to get some nastiness in return.
- You cannot "unsend" an e-mail message. Avoid **flames** or messages that contain strong language and are meant to criticize or provoke. Look over your mail carefully before you send it. Just like any other form of communication, don't e-mail in anger. Give yourself a chance to cool down before you send your message. Writing down your angry thoughts is a great way to get rid of them, but only foolish people press Send instead of Delete!
- Immediately delete any chain letters you receive, and don't pass them along. They use up valuable system resources (including disk space) and may even clog networks.

- Don't send messages intended for one person to all members of a **mailing list**. Similarly, we all enjoy the occasional joke, but don't make a habit of forwarding everything you receive. Don't fill up your friends' and co-workers' in-boxes.

CHAPTER 3

Navigating the World Wide Web

If this book were intended for students of a discipline other than communication, we would begin this chapter by touting the wonders of the Web and its usefulness for those students. Because you are studying human communication, however, we believe it is most appropriate to begin with another topic: namely, the nature of information. More importantly, we believe it is especially relevant to consider whether that information is pushed toward or pulled by those who seek it.

In Chapter 1 we introduced the notion that media can range from "active" to "passive," in terms of how much effort is required by those who use them. Recall also that we suggested that television was one of the most passive media (along with radio), because no effort is required by the viewer to acquire its content. As a result, television and radio can be thought of as "pushing" their content toward the viewer. Keep in mind that, because part of that content is advertising, this idea of pushing ads toward a passive audience has great commercial appeal.

In marked contrast, we have described the newer electronic media, and particularly the WWW, as active media that require some effort from users to acquire the information they desire. The individual who wants information from the Web must find it, read it, decide to save or discard it, and so on. Given this heightened level of activity, those who acquire information from the Web are thought to be "pulling" that information.

This active, thinking approach to information also extends to advertising: if people want information about a product or a service, they must seek it out. The opposite is also true; if you don't want to be exposed to a commercial appeal, you can avoid or bypass it. The ability to avoid commercials, needless to say, does not please advertisers. Accordingly, later in this chapter we will briefly discuss how commercial interests are trying to change the nature of the Web from pull to push. Not surprisingly, the model they hold up as most desirable is the passive medium of television. You might find it interesting to discuss with your class whether such a change in the Web would be good, bad, or uneventful.

ORGANIZATION OF THE WEB

We have already discussed the concept of the client/server relationship several times. Consequently, here we will just urge you to remember that the machine that you are using is the "client" that your Web browser softwáre (Netscape, for example) allows to be connected to thousands of "servers" around the world. Most of the time, this relationship operates without the security safeguards of an ID and password. From time to time, however, you will be required to log on, mostly at commercial sites where either (1) you have paid a fee to obtain valuable information or (2) the business that owns the site wishes to obtain demographic information about those who visit that site. If you are uncomfortable about providing your name and e-mail address to gain entrance, simply move on to another site.

Web Addresses: URLs

Thus far we've been relatively casual about navigating the Web, as in the previous paragraph when we say "simply move on" when you wish to leave the Web page you are currently viewing. Physically, this navigation is done with no more than a click of the mouse on a hyperlink. Despite this physical simplicity, you cannot progress much farther in your mastery of the Web without realizing that each of these links is an address that directs your browser to a precise location on the Internet. Although a browser such as Netscape will do 95% of the work of interpreting these Web addresses, a bit of knowledge on your part can frequently make the difference in whether that last 5% results in success or frustration.

The formal name for an address on the World Wide Web is a **Uniform Resource Locator** or **URL** (pronounced "you-are-el," *not* "earl"). Below is an example of a URL containing the address of the home page of the International Communication Association or ICA:

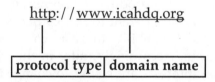

Every URL consists of the two basic parts identified below the ICA address. If you have never seen such an address before, it may look imposing, but when each part is treated separately, their interpretation becomes much simpler.

Protocol Types. The first thing that every URL tells the browser is what type of file or activity the browser is going to encounter at that address. This information is called the file's **protocol**. There are only a few basic types. The initials of the protocol are always followed by a colon (:) and two forward slashes (//). In our Web address for ICA, the protocol for this home page is **http** or **hypertext transfer protocol**. We have defined several of the most basic protocols in the table below.

http://	obtain a file using hypertext transfer
ftp://	obtain a file using file transfer protocol
gopher://	obtain a file on a gopher server
telnet://	open and log on to a telnet server
mailto://	send E-mail to the address in the URL

As new ways to display information are introduced, this list of protocols will no doubt grow larger. For the present, however, these five types will be the most frequent protocols you will encounter.

Domain Name. We introduced domain names in Chapter 2 in our discussion of e-mail addresses. The domain name refers to the particular computer on the Internet that is the server for the desired Web page. In our ongoing example, the ICA home page is located on a computer called "www.icahdq" that is maintained by a nonprofit organization (.org) in the United States (recall: the .us is not needed). As was the case with e-mail, the abbreviation for the organization will change according to the organization's purpose (.edu, .gov, .com), and a country code must be used for computers outside of the United States.

To extend this example, if you wanted information from the home page of the American Broadcasting Company, the URL would be: http://www.abc.com/. If you have been following our discussion so far, you will have no trouble guessing what communication organization you would find at http://www.nytimes.com/. How about the baseball team at http://www.indians.com/? Similarly, you could probably predict what type of information you would find at the URL called http://www.cocacola.com/ or http://www.whitehouse.gov/.

Already, you're getting the hang of it! Before you get too confident, though, you might not guess that http://www.si.edu is the address for the Smithsonian Institution, or that http://www.tucows.com/ is an outstanding site for downloading software from the Web. Fortunately, in these and thousands of other instances, your browser will find these sites with no difficulty.

Directory/File Name. In all of the examples we have listed, there was no directory or file name following the (/). In such instances, the file containing the desired information is located in the very top directory. At such sites, you can navigate further into the site, but you cannot browse higher because you are already at the highest level.

To illustrate such navigation, we need only go to the Web site for the other prominent communication organization, the National Communication Association (NCA). The URL for the home page of NCA is http://www.natcom.org/. Assume, however, that you are interested in possibly becoming a member of NCA. You would click on the hyperlink for Membership and be taken to the URL:

http://www.natcom.org/membership/aboutNCA.htm

To understand this URL, let's work backwards. The file you are seeking in this example is called "aboutNCA.htm." This is an HTML file called "aboutNCA" that is found in a directory labeled "membership." Many Web sites are organized in this manner, that is, with all of the files about a specific topic being located in a separate subdirectory under the main home page for the site. This makes the job of maintaining and updating the site much easier.

After exploring the Web for just awhile, you will become quite used to these addresses, and you will often be able to guess accurately in advance an organization's address. Here is a hint: Some Web sites have such unique addresses that Netscape can locate them with only part of the URL. For example, entering only "nbc" in the location window of the browser (don't forget to hit the Enter key) will expand it to http://www.nbc.com/ and take you directly to the site for the National Broadcasting Company.

MASTERING THE WEB BROWSER

We need to be very clear at the outset of this section. No matter how well we write the next few pages, you will not master the WWW solely by reading this guide. You must sit down at a computer, call up your Web browser, and experiment, practice, explore, mess around, or otherwise become familiar with this software and how it operates. Recognizing that, here we will opt for an overview of the various parts of this browser, rather than overwhelm you with details.

Later, when we discuss class-related activities (such as searching for information), we will expand our discussion and become more detailed. For the present, however, we need to introduce the various parts and components of Netscape.

An Overview of Netscape

Figure 3.1 displays an annotated view of the Netscape window with a blank content area. The most straightforward way to explain the various parts of this software is to begin at the top of this figure and work our way downward.

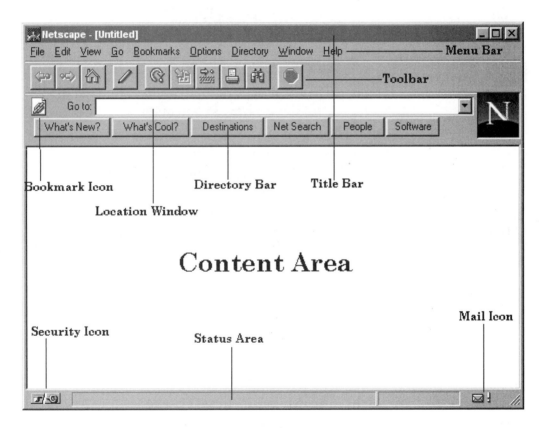

Figure 3.1 (Copyright © 1996 Netscape Communications Corp. Used with permission. All rights reserved. This electronic file or page may not be reprinted or copied without the express written permission of Netscape.)

Title Bar. At the top of each Netscape screen is a bar that displays the title of the Web page you are viewing. Because this is a blank page containing no content, it has no title.

Menu Bar. Regardless of what type of computer you are using to view Netscape, there will always be a Menu bar on the second tier of the window. As with other graphical software, clicking on a menu item will cause a list of possible commands to drop down. Clicking on one of the commands, assuming that it is available, will cause it to be carried out. Because there are so many commands under each menu item, we will use Table 3.1 to briefly summarize their basic functions.

MENU ITEM	COMMANDS IN THAT MENU
File	Open and close windows; open a new browser window; save or print the contents of the current window
Edit	Undo, cut, copy, paste, and find; also a command to "select all" of the window's contents
View	Reload or refresh the current window; load images; view the HTML code that created the current window
Go	Back to the previous page; go forward to a previous page; go to the home page; or select recently viewed pages from a list
Bookmarks	Add the current page as a bookmark at the bottom of the list; open the bookmark list in a separate window; select a bookmark from a list
Options	Customize a variety of Netscape features
Directory	Go to any of a variety of interesting sites provided by the Netscape Corporation. These menu items are exactly the same as the buttons on the Directory bar
Windows	Open Netscape News, Netscape Mail, Bookmarks, Address Book for Mail, or view a history of the sites you have visited during this Netscape session
Help	Receive assistance from the Netscape Corporation in the form of online HTML pages

Table 3.1

Toolbar. Located directly beneath the menu items is the toolbar, each of whose icons performs a single, specific action when it is clicked (only a single click is required). Notice that, in Figure 3.1, several of the icons are "grayed out," thus indicating that their command or function is not available. We will describe these icons in Table 3.2, moving from left to right on the toolbar.

ICON	ACTION ISSUED BY CLICKING ICON
	When this button is active (i.e., not "grayed out"), your browser moves **backward** to the previously viewed page.
	When this button is active, your browser moves **forward** to the previously viewed page.
	Directs your browser to move directly to the **home page** that you have designated in the Options menu. If no home page is designated, the browser moves to the main home page for Netscape.
	Reloads the contents of the current page from the server. This command is useful when editing a Web page (to see how it looks after changes have been made) or when the original attempt to load the page was unsuccessful.
	Loads the images for the current page. This icon is active only when the **Auto Load Images** selection in the Options menu is turned off. Turning this option off will save time when accessing Web pages, but you will not see any images on that page. Clicking this icon will reload the page with those images visible.
	Opens the Location Dialogue box so that you can type the URL of the Web site you wish to visit. You can achieve this same effect by clicking in the **Location Window** and typing in the URL.
	Prints the current Web page.
	Searches for a work or phrase in the current Web page by opening a dialogue box into which you type the text you wish to find.
	Interrupts the loading of the current Web page. When the page is loading, this icon is red (like a stop sigh); when loading is completed, the icon turns gray.

Table 3.2

Other Icons in Netscape. Returning to Figure 3.1 (p. 39), we see three additional icons whose meaning you will need to know. To the left of the Location window is a small icon that resembles a link in a chain [icon]. This is the Bookmark icon. If you move your mouse cursor over this icon, its purpose will be displayed in the Status Area. Double-clicking on this icon will place the URL for the current Web page at the bottom of your bookmark list. When this is used in this manner, it performs exactly as the Add Bookmark command in the Bookmarks menu.

If your bookmarks are displayed in a separate window (by clicking on Show Bookmarks in the Bookmarks menu), you can drag the current URL (by holding the mouse key down and moving the mouse) to the exact location in the bookmark list you wish to place it. We will talk later about the importance of bookmarks, as well as various ways to organize them.

At the bottom of the Netscape window, directly to the right of the Status area, is the Security icon. This icon resembles an old-fashioned key [icon]. Most often, the requests for information you send to Web sites, as well as the replies you receive, are "unsecure." By this, we mean that there is no attempt to **encrypt** or encode the transactions to protect them from hackers or thieves who might try to intercept them along their electronic route. When transactions have no encryption, the Security icon takes the form of a "broken" key.

Some transactions, particularly financial transactions on the Web, require more security. For example, shopping for goods and services online is becoming a more common occurrence. To purchase a product, you fill out a form with pertinent information, including your credit card number. Such transactions are almost always "secure"; your personal information and (especially) your credit card number are encrypted or encoded so that they can be decoded only by the company at the other end of the transaction. Even if hackers were able to intercept your transmission, all they would obtain is gibberish. When Netscape is in this secure mode, the key icon becomes whole, thus signifying that only those with the "key to the code" can make sense out of your information.

Finally, on the other side of the Status Area is the Mail icon. This icon resembles a small envelope [icon]. Clicking on this icon will call the Netscape mail program that was discussed in Chapter 2. In Figure 3.1 (p. 39), you can also see that the envelope icon has an exclamation point to its right. This is a silent message that new mail has arrived since the last time the mailbox was checked. Once you have called up the mail program, this exclamation point will disappear.

Practice, Practice, Practice! Now that you have a passing familiarity with the menus, toolbar, and icons involved, you must sit down with Netscape (or whichever browser your university uses) and practice. Computer skills are learned through the fingertips, not the cortex, so you must put your fingertips to work.

> **Suggestion for practice:** Find the sites mentioned earlier in this chapter. Move around in them and see what's there. Here's a challenge: Try to find the Web pages for the two authors of this book. We'll even give you a hint: you have to start at http://www.udel.edu/, find the Department of Communication, and then find us. Did you imagine we looked like that?

SEARCHING FOR INFORMATION

No matter how adept you become at using a Web browser such as Netscape, your skill will accomplish relatively little if you cannot locate useful and necessary information. The exploration of the WWW can be fun, and it is frequently interesting to hyperlink your way from page to page just to see what you can find.

Similarly, the Web is a great place for recreational pursuits that are unrelated to classes and academics. Remember that you can use those same skills to obtain information about *your* hobby, which should be added motivation to master the art of Web searching.

Information Directories

Some businesses, organizations, and individuals have begun to organize the material on the Internet. These information directories are lists of sites categorized by subject. For those of you who are still exploring what the WWW has to offer, some of these directories could be a good starting point for your search. Just as you might go to the reference room of your school's library and scan the shelves to see what's available on a specific topic, information directories allow you to browse the WWW for information. These directories are particularly useful because they offer shortcuts to a wealth of WWW sites. Each directory is a list of hyperlinks. Just a click on the mouse takes you to potentially useful sites. You don't have to type or even know the URLs.

Yahoo (www.yahoo.com) is perhaps the best-known information directory. Figure 3.2 (p. 44) shows the Yahoo home page. As you can see, it is a collection of hypertext links to various directories of information. As Figure 3.3 (p. 45) shows, clicking on the Government link brings you to another list of subcategories that

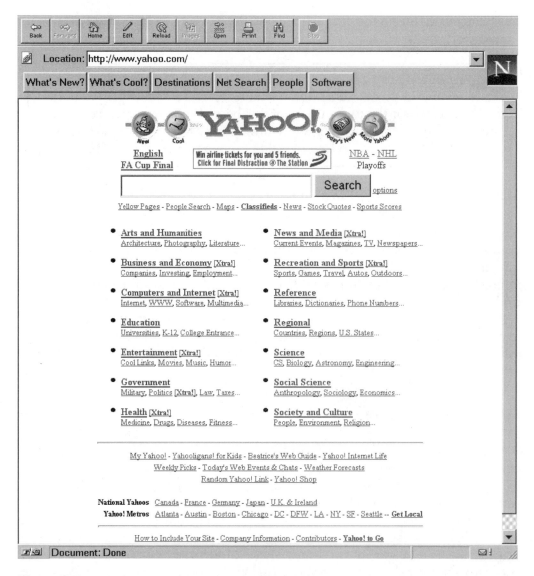

Figure 3.2 (Text and artwork copyright © 1997 by Yahoo! , Inc. All Rights Reserved. Yahoo! and the Yahoo! logo are trademarks of Yahoo!, Inc. Copyright © 1996 Netscape Communications Corp. Used with permission. All Rights Reserved. This electronic file or page may not be reprinted or copied without the express written permission of Netscape.)

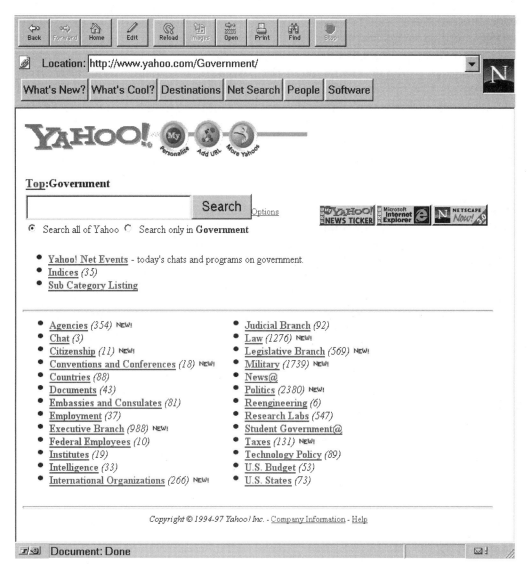

Figure 3.3 (Text and artwork copyright © 1997 by Yahoo! , Inc. All Rights Reserved. Yahoo! and the Yahoo! logo are trademarks of Yahoo!, Inc. Copyright © 1996 Netscape Communications Corp. Used with permission. All Rights Reserved. This electronic file or page may not be reprinted or copied without the express written permission of Netscape.)

each link to more specific resources—all offering information about various government agencies and topics.

We'll discuss WebCrawler (www.webcrawler.com) when we introduce search engines, but as you can see in Figure 3.4 (p. 49), WebCrawler also offers information directories available for browsing. Another directory that is useful for students in communication courses is Galaxy (galaxy.einet.net). It has directories for a variety of topics, from business and commerce to social sciences. There are a variety of directories prepared by businesses on the Internet. We'll include some of these in our Web page for users of this book.

There are also many noncommercial directories on the Web. Several libraries have begun to organize electronic resources by topics. Check out your own school's library. Many nonprofit and educational organizations have compiled lists of Web sites that offer related information. The Banned Books On-Line Web page (http://www.cs.cmu.edu/People/spok/banned-books.html) not only has links to most of the books that are regularly banned, but also has links to other sites that deal with censorship and free speech. One overlooked source for WWW information directories may be your own instructor; more and more teachers are creating course Web pages that include links to useful WWW resources.

Tip: As you are browsing through information directories, remember that the back arrow icon returns you to the previous page. And clicking on the Go menu will show you a list of the pages that you have visited. So, you can jump back to your directories.

Another tip: Later on in this chapter, we will describe how you can create bookmarks to useful sites. You might want to bookmark some of these information directories.

Search Engines

Searching for information on the WWW is made much easier because there are special Web sites designed to do the search for you. On the surface, these sites consist of an uncomplicated form where a user enters the word or phrase—the **search string**—that they wish to find, for example, "speech communication." Behind this deceptively simple interface, however, is a powerful computer program called a **search engine**. By clicking on a nearby button labeled search or submit, this software explores thousands of Web pages looking for the words or phrase that was entered.

In a short period of time (a minute or so at most), the search engine returns a listing of **hyperlinks** to all of the pages found to contain the desired string of characters. To continue our example, searching for the phrase "speech communication" will return a list of over 300 sites that contain those words at least once. Usually, the search engine returns this list in shorter, more manageable pieces (ranging from 10 to 25 entries at a time), but you can certainly page through all 300+ sites if you wish.

There are many search engine sites on the Web (over 20 at last count), some are general and others are devoted to specific topics. Clearly, we cannot discuss them all here, but most are listed in the Appendix at the end of this book.

Given this limitation, we will present one basic yet general search engine called WebCrawler, and another quite comprehensive site entitled MetaCrawler. The selection of these two, however, is *not* a recommendation to use these sites exclusively, but rather a decision based on the size of this book. You may find another search engine to be more suited to your needs, so we encourage you to explore them all before settling on one or two.

WebCrawler. Figure 3.4 (p. 48) displays the home page for the WebCrawler search engine. You can find this site at: http://webcrawler.com/. As we described, the site contains a single box, where you enter the search string, and a submit button. This site also contains a set of 18 predetermined topics that have proven useful and most likely to occur in a search of those general subjects. Finally, you will see advertising for several corporations. This advertising, of course, is what supports the creators of this site so that it is free to you.

Equally important for beginning users of a search engine such as this is the Help button in the top, right-hand corner of the screen. We will later discuss ways to broaden and narrow your searches; the methods for doing this are slightly different for each search engine. The methods for refining searches, however, are always discussed thoroughly in the site's Help pages. Spending a few minutes with these pages is a wise investment of time.

Figure 3.5 (p. 49) presents a partial listing of the results of this search. We can see that 457 "hits" were returned and 25 are displayed on this page (although the figure only shows a few of those). Notice that each of the items in the list is underlined, indicating that it is a hyperlink. Clicking on such an item will take you directly to the site indicated by the listing.

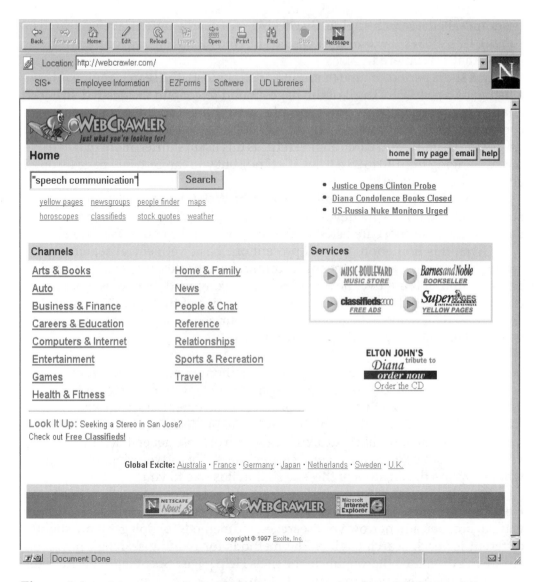

Figure 3.4 (WebCrawler and the WebCrawler Logo are trademarks of Excite, Inc. and may be registered in various jurisdictions. Excite screen display copyright 1995-97 Excite, Inc.)

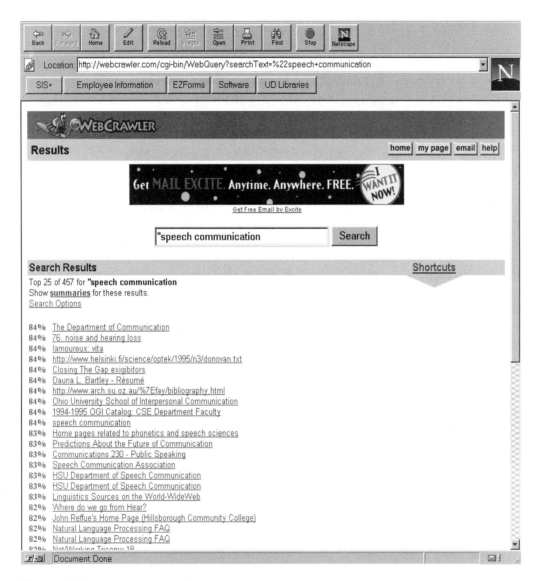

Figure 3.5 (WebCrawler and the WebCrawler Logo are trademarks of Excite, Inc. and may be registered in various jurisdictions. Excite screen display copyright 1995-97 Excite, Inc.)

> **Tip:** In Windows95, clicking on a hyperlink with the right mouse button instead of the left will display a menu. If you "left click" on the item "Open Link in New Browser Window," the linked site will be displayed in a new Netscape window. When you are finished exploring that site, close the window and you will return to your original listing at the same point you where left it.

As our discussion has shown, WebCrawler is a very straightforward search engine that will allow you to find information on a variety of general topics. We will also demonstrate shortly that WebCrawler is one of the simplest search engines for expanding or limiting your searches with special key words. But first we will introduce you to one of the most comprehensive search engines, MetaCrawler.

MetaCrawler. As you begin to explore the pros and cons of various search engines, you will notice that they don't all provide the same results. A search with one engine will provide items that another does not. About that time you will say to yourself, "I wish I could somehow use them all." And with MetaCrawler, you can—well perhaps not "all," but certainly quite a few.

The prefix "meta" is synonymous with the word "about." Thus, "metacommunication" is communication about communication, and the search engine MetaCrawler is a "crawler about crawlers;" or more precisely, a "crawler *of* crawlers." MetaCrawler contains a program that searches other search engines. Moreover, it collates all of the results from numerous other engines, discards the duplicates, and presents only the unique entries from every search. As a result, MetaCrawler is usually more comprehensive and efficient than almost any other search engine.

The main page for the MetaCrawler search engine is shown in Figure 3.6. Its URL is http://www.metacrawler.com/. Note that, besides the space for the search phrase, this site contains other options to control the search. The "buttons" that determine how the search string should be treated (for example, as a phrase, all of these words) are especially useful.

The results of the search using MetaCrawler are presented in Figure 3.7 (p. 52). First, note that only 48 unique results were returned. These are displayed on four pages, each of which contain 10 items and a brief description of each. How can this be "more comprehensive" as we earlier claimed? By default, MetaCrawler limited our search to 10 items per engine, which would have resulted in close to 100 items, but many were discarded as redundant. If we had

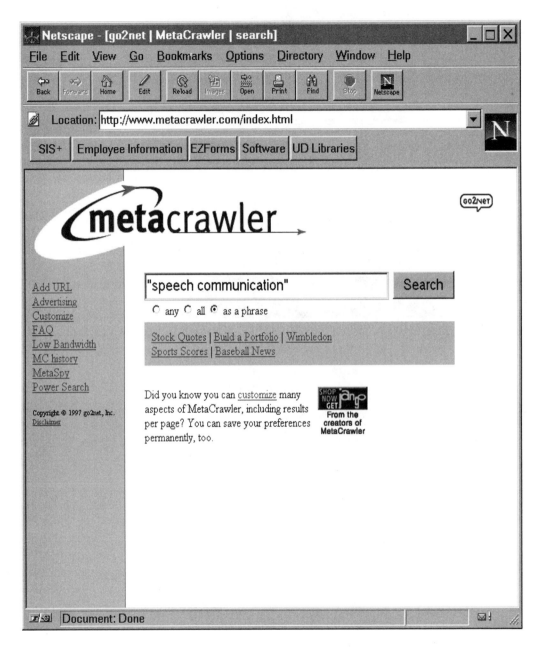

Figure 3.6 (Reprinted with express permission of go2net, Inc.)

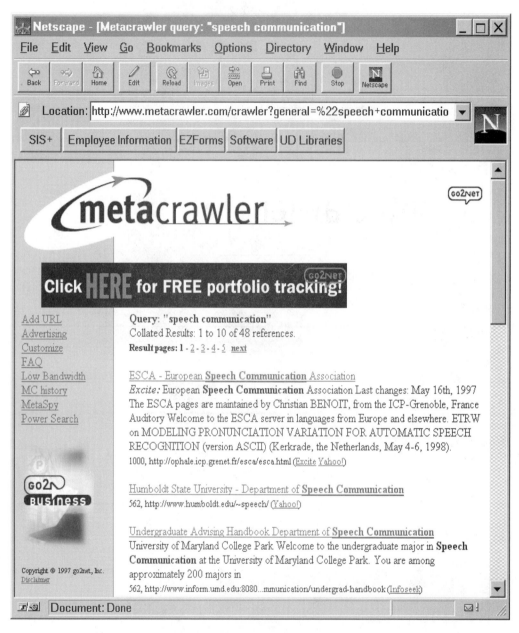

Figure 3.7 (Reprinted with express permission of go2net, Inc.)

conducted our search with the maximum number of items from each site (30 items), the listing of non-redundant items would have totaled 80. Having this many items to explore would certainly keep a person busy for quite some time!

Let us reiterate that these are only two of many search engines that exist on the WWW. Others are being introduced every month. One of your initial tasks in mastering the Web is to try numerous sites using the same search string. Perhaps the best way to locate a wide variety of different search engines is to go to MetaCrawler and insert the phrase, "search engines." Such a search will return almost 40 Web sites that provide listings of various search engines. Try several. Which search engine do *you* like best? That is probably the one you will return to on a regular basis.

Search Strategies

The WWW is like a giant electronic library with massive amounts of information on virtually any topic you can imagine. Some of that information, of course, is worthless, but some is invaluable and it's out there if you can find it.

Unlike a library, however, the Web has no method for organizing this vast storehouse of information. There is no card catalogue, no reference room with helpful librarians to point you in the right direction, and no numbering system for books, articles, government documents, and the like. Accordingly, if you use the Web to discover the informational resources you require, you will need to become adept at sorting through mounds of unwanted material to pinpoint precisely what you want. In short, you are going to need a strategy for searching the Web.

Beginning with a plan, of course, isn't much different from how you would conduct research in a traditional library. Few of us would enter a large university library and aimlessly wander around the shelves hoping to stumble across the books or articles we need. Instead, we would organize a search, perhaps by topic, author or key word in the card catalogue Or perhaps we would consult a reference volume to find articles that address the topic of our search. Whatever method you employ (including asking the librarian), even the use of a traditional library, requires some type of strategy if your search is to be successful.

The same is true for searches on the Web, but the need for a strategy is multiplied many times over. Certainly, the search engines we have described will get you started, but without a plan, they are very blunt instruments, when most often what you need is a finely honed scalpel. What needs sharpening in this instance, however, is not the instrument, but rather your searching skills.

On the Web, search strategies assume one of two forms. Either you will need to focus, limit, or narrow your search to find the relevant information, or you will need to broaden and expand that search. Sometimes you will need to do both at different times in the same search. Accordingly, in the next few sections we will discuss several ways to implement both of these strategies.

Narrowing a Search. We will present four basic ways to narrow a search using a search engine. Keep in mind that all of our examples will apply to the WebCrawler search engine. Although the strategies will be the same for other engines, the exact methods of implementing them may be slightly different. Always look at the Help pages to discover what method is used by a particular search engine.

- *Use phrases instead of words*. Listing several words as the search string will cause the engine to locate Web sites that contain any one of those words. For example, entering the two words, "television" and "violence," will return any page that contains either word, resulting in over 40,000 items. By placing quotation marks around the words, "television violence," however, you are telling the engine to treat these words as a phrase, and only list pages on which those words appear next to each other. In this instance, the number of items returned will be reduced to less than 50.

- *Use specific rather than general words*. Some words are so general that they will generate tens of thousands of hits when entered into a search engine. Entering words such as "program," or "project," not to mention more relevant terms such as "communication," or "speech," will overwhelm you with the number of hits they produce. Somewhere in those thousands of items are the several you are looking for, but good luck trying to find them.

  Instead of these general terms, try more specific words. Perhaps try turning the word into a phrase by preceding it with an adjective. For example, a search on the "Gemini Project" will find much more specific information than either "project" or even "space program." Alternatively, turn a general word into an adjective, such as "communication education," instead of simply "communication." In this latter example, you would have reduced your hits from 44,936 to a more manageable list of 189. Finding the appropriate words or phrases will, no doubt, require some creativity and imagination on your part, but can frequently result in more focused and useful searches.

- *Use the word NOT to eliminate unwanted items.* In the WebCrawler search engine, you can eliminate hits on a specific word or phrase by preceding it with the uppercase word NOT. Other search engines frequently use the minus symbol "–" for the same purpose. For example, searching for the phrase "interpersonal communication" will generate a list of 300+ items, many of which are URLs of academic programs. Following that phrase with the terms NOT School NOT Program NOT Department will cut the list by more than half.

- *Use the word AND to force the inclusion of limiting words.* In some instances, including additional terms can serve to limit a search. In this case, the use of the term "AND" in WebCrawler (or the "+" sign in other engines), will force the search to be more selective. For example, searching on the basic term "persuasion" will generate a list of over 1,400 items that contain that word. Many of these—for example, numerous references to Jane Austen's (1818) novel, *Persuasion*—are not relevant for someone who is interested in human communication. By adding the word "communication" to the search string (persuasion AND communication), the list is reduced to 243. If we go one step further and include the term "Department" (e.g., persuasion AND communication AND Department), the list is reduced to a mere 74 items. Now we can do some serious browsing on our main topic of interest!

Expanding a Search. Our experience with Web searches has rarely involved too little information. On the contrary, we generally encounter the types of results discussed previously, where our search strings generate thousands of hits and we must take steps to reduce their number.

Once in a great while, however, you will enter a search string and no items (or very few) will be returned. When this happens, you will find it useful to have a few strategies for enlarging your search to actually encompass more information. Given the infrequency with which these strategies are required, we will present them rather briefly.

- *Use synonyms to search for the same topic.* In some ways, this is the reverse of the strategy we outlined above for limiting a search. Nevertheless, using the right word can often lead to an abundance of material; the wrong search string might generate nothing. If searching for "encoder" produces an empty list, try "speaker," "sender," or "communicator." Similarly, a search for the renowned social psychologist Leon Festinger will produce no hits, but substituting the name of his most famous theory, "cognitive dissonance," will result in a list of 37 items.

Again, there are no hard-and-fast rules about which synonyms will work. Frequently, however, a bit of ingenuity will start you on your way to a successful search.

- *Use the terms AND as well as OR to expand your search.* Again, some repeat advice: Remember that the use of "AND" forces a word or phrase to be included in the search, but the term "OR" will generate a hit on either item. As an example, a search for the phrase "communicator credibility" will produce a list with no entries. In contrast, changing the phrase slightly to "communication AND credibility" will produce 542 items. What a difference!

- *Check (or alter) your spelling.* This seems too elementary to mention, but you would be surprised how many times a simple error of typing will foil an otherwise well-planned search. Computers are basically dumb, and they will search for exactly the word or phrase you provide—no more, no less. A misspelled search string will launch a misspelled search, and the outcome will be useless.

> **Tip:** You may spell a word accurately, but it is often still not the right word. The word "video" is not the same as "videos," and "communication" and "communications" will not generate the same list. When in doubt, try several variations of singular and plural. Once in a while you'll get lucky!

General Advice on Searching. There are two general pieces of advice that we have found useful in conducting searches, but neither fits into the categories we have outlined above. First, *learn from your searches!* Look carefully at the list of items you have generated. Are these what you want? If not, what topics need to be included or excluded? For example, if a search for "persuasion" produces numerous references to Jane Austen's novel, conduct a second search, but eliminate "Jane" by use of the word NOT. Computers may be dumb, but you're not! Think about what you're doing and try, try again.

Our second piece of advice is a bit more abstract, but nonetheless useful. Many times a search will identify a Web page that by itself is not useful but seems to be in the middle of a site that holds promise. Look for links to the site's home page. Well-maintained Web sites always have them, and they can take you right where you want to go.

> **Tip:** When there is no direct link to the home page, work "backward" into the site by placing your cursor in the Location box (this will require two clicks) and deleting the text from the end of the URL back to the first forward slash (/). Then hit Enter. You will have moved up a level in the site, where you will most likely see a listing of the pages that site contains. Try a few. Obviously, you're exploring here, but you'd be surprised how a little perseverance can pay off.

STORING INFORMATION FOR LATER USE

Chances are good that if you've gone to the trouble of conducting a serious search of the Web, you will want to keep a record of what you've found. We will suggest four alternative ways to store permanently the information you have obtained. We will also include a fifth section with some advice about capturing and downloading graphics.

Bookmarks

The easiest and least expensive (because it uses no paper) way of keeping track of useful Web sites is to add them to your **bookmarks**. As we described in our earlier overview of the Netscape browser, you can make a URL into a bookmark by clicking on either (1) the Bookmark icon ( ) next to the Location Box, or (2) the Bookmarks menu and selecting "Add Bookmark." Once a bookmark is established, clicking on it will take you directly to the Web site it represents.

Given how easy it is to make bookmarks, let's spend the majority of this section discussing ways to organize bookmarks once you have saved them. This can become an important concern, because if you begin to bookmark many sites (a good idea), you will soon have a list of dozens or even hundred of sites. Unless you have an ongoing plan for organizing these sites, however, your efforts will result in little more than chaos. We actually know people who end up having to search their own bookmarks. Now that's disorganized!

The key to the effective organization of your bookmarks is much the same as our advice in Chapter 2 about storing and organizing e-mail: create folders that contain bookmarks on similar topics. First, go to the Bookmarks menu and select "Go to Bookmarks." Your bookmarks will appear in a window that looks similar to that displayed in Figure 3.8. Your window, however, may not yet have any folders displayed, but we are about to remedy that.

Go to the Item menu and select the entry labeled Insert Folder. Currently, the name you give the folder is not crucial, but as you acquire more bookmarks, you will want these names to be meaningful. You can get a sense of various folder names by looking at the two figures below.

As you acquire new bookmarks, these will automatically be placed at the bottom of the list. To place them in the appropriate folder, drag and drop them on that folder. That's it: You're already starting to organize your life on the Web. You will probably begin with only a few major folders, but as time passes, do not hesitate to create more to handle new topics.

Once you have established several useful folders, you merely click on the small "+" symbol to open one. The bookmarks it contains are then displayed and you can click directly on them to call up that Web site. This is displayed in Figure 3.9, where the Searching folder has been opened to reveal several alternatives for locating material on the Internet. If you find yourself searching the Web on a regular basis, you may wish to create a similar folder.

Finally, what about unused or outdated bookmarks? If at any point you wish to delete a bookmark or a folder (and sooner or later you will), just select the item you wish to discard and hit the Delete key. Be careful, because once it's gone, it's gone for good.

> **Tip:** Netscape also allows you to put folders inside of folders (this is called "nesting"), thus letting you divide your bookmarks into subtopics. To do this, open the folder as just described, and insert another folder. It couldn't be simpler!

Now that you realize how easy it is to make folders and organize your bookmarks, there is only one final step: You must actually do it! We know from experience how easy it is to forget to constantly monitor your bookmarks or, more likely, put it off until you have more time. The result of this procrastination will almost always be the chaotic mess we described earlier. Stay on top of your bookmarks, and they'll be there when you need them.

Printing

A second option for permanently storing the results of your Web searches is to send the pages to your printer. The easiest way to do this is to click on the Print

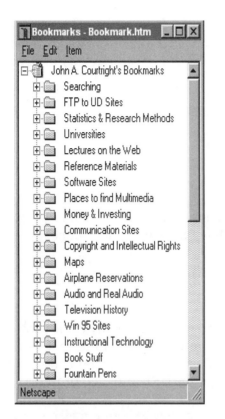 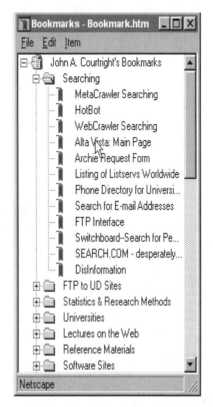

Figure 3.8   **Figure 3.9**

icon. You can also open the File menu and click on the Print item. In either case, a Print Information box will appear. Just click OK. You will receive a relatively faithful representation of the Web page you were viewing (albeit usually in black and white).

A second, perhaps more interesting issue involves the question: when should you print? One of the advantages of the Web, of course, is the abundance of resources that exist in electronic form. To trade these for a large stack of paper would seem to be defeating the entire purpose of the Internet. Hence, a bit of discretion is required.

Before you print, think about the nature of the information you are viewing and consider how you plan to use it. If you have discovered a standard, established Web site (one that is likely to be there permanently), a bookmark is probably the wiser option. Not only can you visit the site whenever you want or need to, but you also forego having to transport or store reams of expensive paper.

In contrast, if you are viewing a lengthy, textual document (for example, a research article), you may find it more beneficial to have a hard copy. You can then read it at your convenience, highlight it, and even write comments in the margins. Moreover, if you plan to use this document to help you write your own paper or report, having a printed copy is clearly preferable. The alternative is constantly switching back and forth between Netscape and your word processor—definitely a hassle.

With a bit of experience, you will probably develop your own rules of thumb for printing versus bookmarking. Both have their uses, but neither should be used routinely without thought.

Mailing Web Pages

When working with others on a project, you will occasionally come across Web pages that you wish to share with the other members of your team. One option, of course, is to copy and paste the URL into your mail program and send it to your coworkers. They will then have to enter the URL into their browser to view that page.

One alternative is to attach the entire Web page to your e-mail message and send it along with the URL. Netscape allows you to accomplish this by clicking on the File menu and selecting the item labeled Mail Web Page. The Netscape mail program then opens up, and the Web page you are viewing is automatically attached to your message. You need only enter the address of the receiver and any message you wish to accompany the attachment.

Whether this is a useful method of sharing information depends almost totally on the type of mail program that will be used by the receiver of your message. If he or she is using a mainframe program where handling attachments is cumbersome, then this approach is probably more trouble (to them) than it's worth. By the time your friend or coworker goes through the several steps of saving, downloading, etc., they could have entered the URL directly into the Location box.

In contrast, if your receiver has a PC-based mail program or, especially if he or she uses the built-in Netscape mail program, this approach has several benefits.

The attached Web page is automatically transferred to their computer, and it can be easily opened with a browser. With the Netscape program the Web page is both transferred and displayed right in the mail window. This is about as simple as it gets.

As our comments would suggest, before using this approach to share information with others, you should make an effort to determine (1) what type of information they would prefer, the URL or the entire page, and (2) what type of mail program they routinely use. You might even try a bit of persuasion to move them off of that antiquated mainframe program and onto one that is located on their own computer. The same goes for you: You'll find that the investment will pay off many times over.

Copy and Paste Functions

One observation we have made is that most people, ourselves included, use materials on the Web similarly to how they employ printed material. Accordingly, while we frequently have need of a short quotation, a line or two of text, or even a particularly useful graphic, we really don't make use of an entire Web page any more often than we would quote an entire book.

With this in mind, we suggest that one of the most useful ways of storing and using information from the Web is to (1) copy it to the system clipboard, and then (2) paste it into your document or presentation at the appropriate place (with proper citation, of course).

The procedure for accomplishing this is basically the same as copying and pasting material between any two Mac or Windows-based programs. First, highlight the material you wish to copy by dragging your mouse cursor across it. Then go to the Edit menu and select the Copy. The material is then placed directly on your computer's clipboard.

Pasting, of course, is just the reverse. Call up the second program (for example, your word processor), select the point in your document where you wish the material to be placed, go to the Edit menu in that program, and select Paste. Almost like magic, the material you just copied instantaneously appears. In many cases, however, the formatting that you saw in the browser is lost when you paste the material into the new program. Hence, you may have to tinker a bit to obtain just the look you want, but at least you saved yourself from having to enter all of that material by hand.

Downloading Graphics

What attracts most of us to the Web is its visual nature: the stunning graphics, the beautiful pictures, the useful charts, and so forth. Given these attractions, it is not surprising that often what we want to obtain from a Web page is one of those graphical elements. Perhaps we want an image to include in a multimedia presentation, or maybe we need just the right chart to make a point persuasively in our research paper. At such times, we decidedly *don't* need the entire Web page, and we aren't interested in the text. So how do we capture just that one, special image?

Fortunately, with Netscape the answer is: easily. To select and download (capture) an image using Netscape, first move your cursor directly over the image. Next, click on the image with the *right* mouse button (Mac users obviously cannot employ this shortcut). A menu with several options immediately appears on the screen. Select the item labeled "Save Image As." A window will then appear asking where on your computer you wish to save this image. Provide a location, click on OK, and the image will be downloaded and stored.

Tip: We encourage you to create a special folder or directory to use exclusively for downloading or storing images from the Web. By having all of these images in the same place, you won't lose track of them—a distinct possibility if you scatter them around your hard disk.

ETHICS OF USING THE WORLD WIDE WEB

Our decision to discuss the ethics of using the Web immediately after the section on permanently storing information was hardly an accident. Although we have repeatedly touted the wealth of information on the Web, we must also assert emphatically that virtually all of that information belongs to somebody else. As a result, those who use it must adhere to a set of ethical practices.

The bulk of these practices can be presented and discussed under one of two headings: (1) copyright laws and (2) citation practices. These are not separate concerns. Nevertheless, we will treat them individually, because one involves legal issues, and the other involves the topic of scholarly ethics, namely plagiarism.

Copyright Laws

We must begin this section by declaring loudly that we are not lawyers and that nothing we write here should be interpreted as legal advice. In fact, we hope that as a result of a basic understanding of copyright issues and following the laws in this area, you will never need a lawyer to defend you against a charge of copyright infringement. If you follow a few simple rules and use a bit of common sense, you will encounter no trouble.

When using material from the Internet, we believe the only prudent way to proceed is to assume that everything is formally and legally copyrighted. This includes text, pictures, logos, graphics . . . everything! Often, of course, this assumption will be inaccurate, but unless you enjoy nasty surprises (usually in the form of a threatening letter from an attorney), treating all material as though it is copyrighted is the only sensible way to proceed.

Copyright Defined. The next logical question then becomes: What does the assumption of copyright mean? Simply stated, *the individual or corporation holding a copyright has exclusive rights to the use of the copyrighted material.* The copyright holder, therefore, has the right to copy, distribute, perform, display, or sell the material. These rights are "exclusive," meaning that no one else can do any of these things to or with the material without the permission of the copyright holder.

Exceptions: Fair Use. Despite this assignment of "exclusive rights," the copyright laws recognize the need for an open, democratic society to discuss, debate, and disagree with ideas, even when they appear in copyrighted material. Such discussion and debate, of course, frequently require the reproduction of small amounts of the original material. Moreover, in instances where there is disagreement with the writer of the original material (this also includes satire and parody), the copyright holder is not likely to grant permission to be quoted.

To reconcile this potential conflict, the copyright laws include a provision for "fair use." This exception allow scholars to quote *brief* passages from a work, whether traditional or electronic, for the purpose of comment, discussion, criticism, etc. This fair use exception also extends to pictures, images, and other visual works. As a student, you fall under this exception when you are using written or Web-based material for your class assignments or papers.

The key term in the previous paragraph is "brief," and much discussion and many court cases have failed to define precisely what that term means. One or two carefully chosen sentences will not cause a problem, but quoting many pages will likely cross the line. In between is a very murky legal area. A student's honest misjudgment about the quantity of quoted material will seldom result in a lawsuit; after all, learning what is appropriate is the essence of being a student. In contrast, making the same mistake a few years from now when you are considered a "professional" may produce a different, more undesirable outcome. Our advice, therefore, is to practice being cautious now, and extend that caution into your professional life.

The other component of fair use that affects you as a student is the provision that allows photocopying for noncommercial research. You are not required to obtain permission to make a single copy of articles, book chapters, Web pages, and so forth, as along as they relate directly to your classes. You may be glad to know that you weren't breaking the law when you copied all of the articles that you checked out of the Reserve Room in the library.

In contrast, it is not considered fair use to make copies of any type of copyrighted material for your personal enjoyment. That's right, making tapes for your car stereo is considered illegal. Similarly, you are breaking the copyright law when you copy an entire work to avoid buying it; this deprives the author (composer, artist, company, etc.) of their "exclusive right" to profit from their work. Hence, if you're reading a photocopy of this book, send us a check immediately and we'll cancel the police raid that is scheduled for your apartment :-).

Citation Practices

This section will be brief and straightforward. Our position is simple: whenever you use the ideas of another person, you must give that individual the credit. Regardless whether the work is copyrighted or not, whether the ideas are direct quotations or paraphrases, or whether the material comes from the Web or more traditional media, presenting the ideas of another as if they were your own is considered serious academic misconduct.

Accordingly, when you use material from a Web page—any type of material—you must give the author or artist credit through the use of a citation. This requirement is really no different than citing the author of a book or the artist who drew a picture. The need to cite also relates to the fair use provisions we discussed earlier: using brief portions of copyrighted material is only considered fair use if the author receives the appropriate credit.

One notable difference between citing traditional material and citing Web-based resources is the actual form or style of the citation. Obviously, a Web page doesn't have a page number, or a publisher, or a volume number. As a result, the traditional styles we might use for footnotes or endnotes don't translate very well to the Web.

In Chapter 6, we will present two different styles for including citations from the Internet. One approach is suggested by the Modern Language Association (MLA); the other is presented by the American Psychological Association (APA). Both are recognized and accepted styles for both traditional and electronic citations. Your instructor or department may have a policy or preference about which to use. If not, compare the styles presented in Chapter 6 (as well as the Web sites listed there), and pick the one that seems most comfortable to you.

CONCLUSION: PUSH VERSUS PULL REVISITED

At the beginning of this chapter, we briefly discussed the nature of information and suggested that a useful distinction was whether that information was *pushed toward* or *pulled by* the user. Recall that, in its very short life span, the Web has always been a medium that required the user to engage actively in the discovery of information and, subsequently, to pull that information to their computer.

There is ample evidence that this approach is about to change. In fact, in the short time that it took us to write this chapter, we have read more than one dozen articles—in both the general press and specialized computer publications—commenting on plans to change the Web from pull to push. As we suggested earlier, this change is prompted by companies who want their advertising to be pushed to your computer screen just as television commercials accompany programming content.

We will refrain from commenting on whether we believe this change will be good or bad. Assuming you have followed our advice and have practiced diligently, you will now have experienced firsthand the activities associated with pulling information. Whether you are willing to trade the effort of actively acquiring information for a more passive approach that includes prominently placed advertisements is something you need to consider.

This change, whether you favor it or not, is really about much more than the inclusion of ads in the content of Web pages. To the contrary, the shift from pull to push represents a fundamental change in the nature of the medium. If you doubt that, imagine the opposite shift in the nature of television, from push to pull. How would television be altered if there were no ads, but instead we had to search actively and regularly to find the programs we wanted to watch? Would viewership decline? Increase? Would the proverbial "couch potatoes" long for the days when they simply reclined in their easy chairs and when operating the remote control was their only form of activity?

Frankly, we don't know the answers to these questions either, but for students of human communication we think they are worth asking. Make no mistake: the Web is changing and will likely change even more. None of us can halt or even control these changes (even if we wanted to), but our interest in communication should prompt us to think about and discuss them.

So . . . stay tuned, or in this case, stay logged on. We are in the midst of some very interesting times!

CHAPTER 4

Using Listservs and Newsgroups

In this chapter we will discuss how you can use the Internet to communicate with large groups of people. Although e-mail enables us to use the Internet to communicate person-to-person, listservs and newsgroups facilitate a one-to-many mode of communication. With both listservs and newsgroups, you will be able to exchange ideas and information with others who share your interests—across the United States and even across the world. Listservs are really automated mailing lists that allow individuals to send e-mail to a large group of subscribers (the **server** mails to the entire list). Newsgroups, on the other hand, are the "bulletin boards" of the Internet. Interested users go to the newsgroups to read the postings or messages placed on the newsgroups by other users. Although listservs and newsgroups are very much alike in function and purpose, there are some important differences between the two.

First, listservs and newsgroups differ along the active/passive continuum. Listservs are a more passive form of communication. Once subscribers have taken the active step to subscribe to a listserv, they can sit back and wait for messages to be mailed automatically to their in-boxes. In contrast, newsgroups are a more active communication mode. If newsgroup subscribers wants to catch up with newsgroup postings, they must make the extra effort to log on to the newsgroup. Listservs are like mail delivered directly to your door. Newsgroups are like bulletin boards that you go to post or read messages.

Another difference between listservs and newsgroups is the audience. Because the software that mails listserv messages needs to know the addresses of its subscribers, it's possible to get a list of all subscribers. Newsgroup audiences are more anonymous. Unless a newsgroup is private or dedicated to a specific purpose, it would be impossible to get a list of everyone who reads the postings.

Finally, listservs are easier to access and use effectively. If you've mastered the simple steps for reading and sending mail, you will be able to read and send listserv messages. Newsgroups are not complicated or difficult, but they require a newsreader program and a few new techniques.

LISTSERVS

Listservs, or mailing lists, are a form of group discussion over the Internet. As you will see, they are an extension of electronic mail. All listserv messages are publicly available to all subscribers. Listservs, however, are a more passive variation of Internet group communication. Newsgroups require you to check in to read the postings; listservs, on the other hand, deliver all messages automatically to your electronic mail in-box.

Listservs serve subscribers with similar interests. Some of these groups can be as diverse as the audiences of popular television programs. One of the largest mailing lists, for example, is Dave Letterman's Top 10 List. Other listservs are more specialized and attract a much smaller group of subscribers. Debaters, for example, might be interested in subscribing to CEDA-L, which covers discussion about intercollegiate forensics. A still smaller group might be interested in subscribing to Commstud, a listserv that connects alumni of Kent State University's graduate program.

Similarly, many universities set up short-term listservs that facilitate communication among students enrolled in specific courses. When the two authors of this book needed to contact our students in the class we team-teach, we just sent mail to comm418-010-97s@udel.edu, and all the students enrolled in COMM 418 (Broadcast Television History), section 10, Spring 1997, received the message. (Note: At the end of each semester, class listservs are deactivated, so don't even bother to try.)

Communication professionals have several listservs available. The Mass Communication Division of the National Communication Association (NCA) uses a listserv to distribute its electronic newsletter. NCA also uses a listserv to distribute *CRTNET*, the *Communication, Research, and Theory Newsletter*. The Communication Institute of Online Scholarship (CIOS) maintains 25 mailing lists (called "hotlines") about a variety of communication-related topics including: health communication, mass communication and new technologies, interpersonal communication, family communication, intercultural communication, gender and communication, and rhetoric, persuasion, and social movements. We include information about a selection of useful communication listservs on this book's own Web site.

As you can see, listservs can be a very useful and efficient way to communicate. There are tens of thousands of listservs about thousands of different topics—from aroma therapy to zymurgy. You are sure to find a mailing list about something that interests you. Listservs are an easy way to contact, share information with, and request advice from people with specialized knowledge. Moreover, receiving regular mail from people who share your interests can perk up your day. But be careful: Some listservs are quite active. Receiving over 100 messages a day is not uncommon. And some listservs (especially ones that don't screen messages for their value or interest) tend to distribute trivial messages that aren't worth the time they take to read.

Both of us have enthusiastically subscribed to mailing lists and anticipated interesting and useful mail. Instead we found our in-boxes filled with so many messages that we couldn't take the time to separate the good from the bad or the ugly. Our only alternative was to unsubscribe.

Finding Listservs

Finding a listserv that suits you can be as easy as clicking on your World Wide Web browser icon. One strategy for finding a listserv is to use one of the search engines described in Chapter 3 to search for terms relevant to your interests. Several of the search engines will also display listservs. This strategy may not be the best way to find the full range of listservs, however.

There are several sites on the Internet that index listservs on every conceivable topic. Liszt (http://www.liszt.com/), for example, maintains a database of more than 50,000 lists. Liszt lets users browse by topic, but its own search engine locates more lists by title. Tile.net (http://www.tile.net/) is another good source for listservs. Tile.net lets you browse lists organized by title, subject, description, country, and sponsor. Both Liszt and Tile.net provide some information about individual listservs, and you can use their e-mail forms to subscribe immediately to any list. We've included several other Web site resources for listservs on this book's Web page.

How to Join a Listserv

Joining a listserv is as easy as sending mail. Just send e-mail to the list's administrative address. Your message is simple: Subscribe <list name> <your name>. So, if you wanted to subscribe to *CRTNET*, you would send the following message to CRTNET@scassn.org:

subscribe CRTNET

You should receive an e-mail message confirming your subscription quite quickly—usually in less than a day, and more often in less than one hour. Make a folder for listserv mail (as we recommended in Chapter 2) and *save that message!* It will be a polite welcome to the list, but more importantly, it includes information that you may need later on. The message will tell you how to post messages, how to unsubscribe (or leave the listserv) and how to access archived messages. Again, *save that message!*

After you have joined, the listserv will send messages directly to your mail program's in-box. Read, delete, reply, forward, and save listserv messages just as you would with regular e-mail messages.

Managing Your Listservs

Sending messages to a listserv is as easy as sending e-mail. We suggest that you add the address of the listserv to your address book. Then simply compose your message and send it to the listserv.

At this point we would remind you of our admonition in Chapter 1 that mailing lists are public communication. Your message will be read by the list's subscribers and can also be forwarded to nonsubscribers. Our best advice is to send no messages that you would be embarrassed to have widely circulated. The likelihood is high that they will be.

Warning! A list's distribution (group) address and subscription (administrative) address are two different addresses. You do not post messages to the subscription address, and you do not subscribe by sending a message to the distribution address. We have too often seen mailing list messages that read "subscribe." Don't embarrass yourself by using the wrong address.

Sometimes, you may find it inconvenient to receive and read listserv messages. There are several ways to manage listserv mail. First, use your mail program's filters to sort your mail and send listserv mailings to a specified folder. This will keep your in-box clear and you can go to the listserv folder to read messages at your convenience. Another simple suggestion is to examine your in-box "subject" listings and discard messages that have no interest to you.

Finally, most listservs allow subscribers to switch to **digest** mode. In this mode, the listserv will send messages to you only once a day, so you can receive these mailings at a more convenient time. You may also want to suspend your subscription, to temporarily stop receiving listserv mailings. This is a useful way to keep your in-box unclogged while you are on vacation. Simply resume your subscription when it is convenient. Check your listserv's welcome message (you saved it, didn't you?) for the correct way to request digest modes or to suspend and resume your subscription.

You may find, though, that your listserv subscription is no longer useful. The list may become inactive, too active, or the information no longer interesting, and you may want to leave the list.

How to Leave a Listserv

Leaving a listserv is as easy as subscribing. Send mail to the listserv administrative address. The message is simple: Unsubscribe <list name> <your name>. So, if you wanted to unsubscribe to *CRTNET*, you would send the following message to CRTNET@scassn.org:

unsubscribe CRTNET

NEWSGROUPS

Newsgroups are online discussion groups organized around specific topics. Newsgroups allow people with similar interests to share, discuss, and debate ideas and information. These are the "bulletin boards" of the Internet. These discussion groups reside on **servers**, or computers that store the various contributions. Subscribers use specialized **client** programs, called newsreaders, to go to those servers and deliver the newsgroup articles, or postings, to their home computers. Newsgroups are the more active form of one-to-many communication on the Internet.

The most widely available newsgroups are on Usenet, a worldwide newsgroup distribution system that was developed for mainframe computers in the late 1970s. Now, newsgroups are so popular that there are now many other sources, but these newsgroups may not always be accessible to everyone. Many commercial Internet service providers, for example, offer discussion "forums" for their subscribers that are identical in form and function to Usenet newsgroups. And many universities provide server space for very specialized newsgroups to serve university and academic groups. Both of the authors of this book, for example, have set up short-term newsgroups to allow students in certain classes to discuss course-related material.

All newsgroups have fairly standard names that describe quite well the subject of the newsgroup. Like e-mail addresses, there are some standard signals for types of newsgroups. If the name of a newsgroup begins with "comp," its discussion will focus on computer-related topics; if it begins with "news," it will cover network topics. Other newsgroups might begin with "rec" (recreational activities), "sci" (science-related topics), "soc" (social and/or political discussions), "talk" (debate about controversial topics), and "misc" (anything that is not covered by the other types of newsgroups). All "alt" newsgroups, focus on "alternative" topics, some of which might be fairly controversial (alt.drugs) or simply topical (alt.fan.oj-simpson). So, a newsgroup whose name is rec.arts.tv.soap.misc includes postings of interest to soap opera viewers. And, alt.sports.baseball.cleve-indians covers discussion of the Cleveland Indians. What do you think the readers of the newsgroup rec.music.phish are interested in?

Finding Newsgroups

There are newsgroups for virtually any topic imaginable. Some newsgroups are instrumental and can provide support or work-related information (for example, alt.support.depression or misc.taxes.moderated). Others are purely recreational (rec.crafts.textiles.yarn or alt.tv.mst3k). There is no way to know exactly how many newsgroups exist, but some estimate that there are now as many as 17,000 active newsgroups on line. With all those newsgroups on the Internet, it's not difficult to find ones that might interest you.

Again, finding a newsgroup is as easy as hopping on the World Wide Web. The Liszt and Tile.net web sites that we suggested as sources for listservs are also comprehensive resources for locating newsgroups by title and topic. Other newsgroup sources are the *Usenet Info Center Launch Pad,* the *Internet Newsgroups,* and *Deja News.* All these sites include search engines so that you can find a newsgroup to interest you. But be careful: many of your searches will turn up newsgroups with limited utility or accessibility, such as those set up specifically for class discussion.

Figure 4.1 shows you how easy it is to search using *Deja News* forms. The URLs for these sites are included on this book's own Web page.

Newsreader Programs

All newsgroups are collections of files submitted by people across the Internet. Once those files are stored on the newsgroup server, anyone with access to the

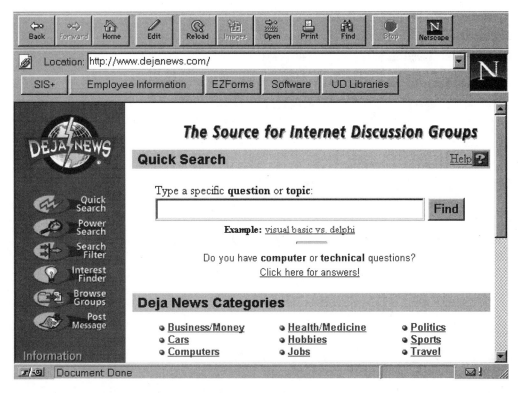

Figure 4.1 (Courtesy of DejaNews, Inc.)

server can read the postings. When you decide that you want to read newsgroup postings, you will need to use a newsreader program. A newsreader is specialized software that retrieves the postings from the newsgroup server, delivers the postings to your terminal, and sends and posts your own messages on the newsgroup server.

There are a variety of newsreaders; the one that you use will depend on your Internet account. Just as most students use the mail program provided by their school's computer system, most students also use the school's newsreader program. Newsreaders like trn, nn, and tin are perfectly serviceable but clumsy programs. Like any Unix-based program, they have no mouse support, no sophisticated word-processing features, and no easy way to attach graphic and multimedia files. But they are available, free, technically supported, and already connected to your school's news server. The commands may seem complicated to students who are used to Windows or a Mac system, but they are usually

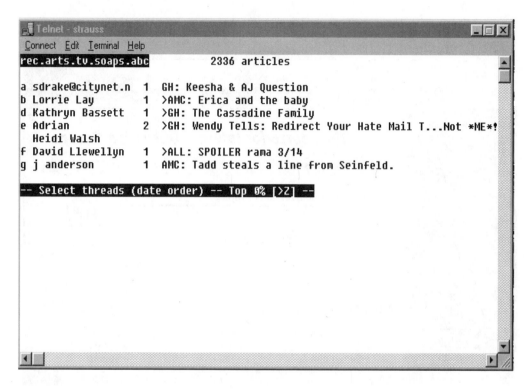

Figure 4.2 (Screen shot reprinted with permission from Microsoft Corporation.)

summarized at the bottom of each screen. Figure 4.2 shows the trn newsreader program that is available on our own university's mainframe.

Several **freeware** and **shareware** newsreaders are available for downloading from the Web. In Chapter 5 we'll give you instructions for FTP-ing programs like Free Agent and NewsXpress. If you have access to a computer connected directly to the Internet, you might want to consider one of these programs. They use all the capabilities of your computer (including mouse support), handle multimedia attachments easily, and may even allow you to store newsgroup postings to read off line. This last feature may be especially useful if you subscribe to an Internet service provider that charges you for the amount of time that you are connected.

The authors of this book have found that one of the easiest ways to access newsgroups is through browser programs. We both use Netscape News to access and manage our newsreading. As you learned in Chapter 3, Netscape is readily available and easy to use, so we will use Netscape's newsreader for most of our examples throughout this chapter. Accessing Netscape's newsreader is easy: just pull down the Window menu and click on Netscape News. In the Options menu, click on Mail and News Preferences. Fill in the information on the Identity screen, which asks for your name and e-mail address, and on the "servers" screen, which asks the location of your mail and news server. If you aren't sure how to list those, check with someone from your Internet service provider. Once those screens are filled in, you're ready to go! Figure 4.3 (p. 76) shows one of our completed News Preferences screens.

The Basics of Newsgroups

No matter which newsreader you use, the basic steps for reading, subscribing, and posting to newsgroups will be the same. Specific commands for different newsreaders do vary, though. If you need help, look on your computer screen. On mainframe computers, commands are usually summarized on the bottom of the screen. With Windows and Mac systems, click on Help for assistance.

Bringing the Newsgroup Postings to You. Remember that newsgroups are a more active form of one-to-many communication on the Internet. You will need to bring the newsgroup postings to your own computer terminal. Your newsreader will do this for you, but you will have to tell it which newsgroups to collect. If you are using your WWW browser as your newsreader, getting newsgroups is easy. If you know the name of the newsgroup you want, click on Add Newsgroup in the File menu and type the name in the form. Your browser will then deliver all of that newsgroup's postings to your screen for you to read. Enter the name carefully. Any typing errors will make your browser return an error message.

If you have been searching for newsgroups using one of the searchable Web sites, clicking on the link to the newsgroup will automatically cause your newsreader to bring that newsgroup's postings to you.

Notice that using your browser as a newsreader allows you to be very selective in the newsgroups that you access. Just like the rest of the World Wide Web, you "pull" the newsgroups to you.

Some mainframe newsreaders use more of a "push" strategy. Our university's mainframe newsreader, trn, begins each newsreading session by listing all new newsgroups that have been started since the user last logged on, whether he or she is interested in seeing the list or not. The program then asks if

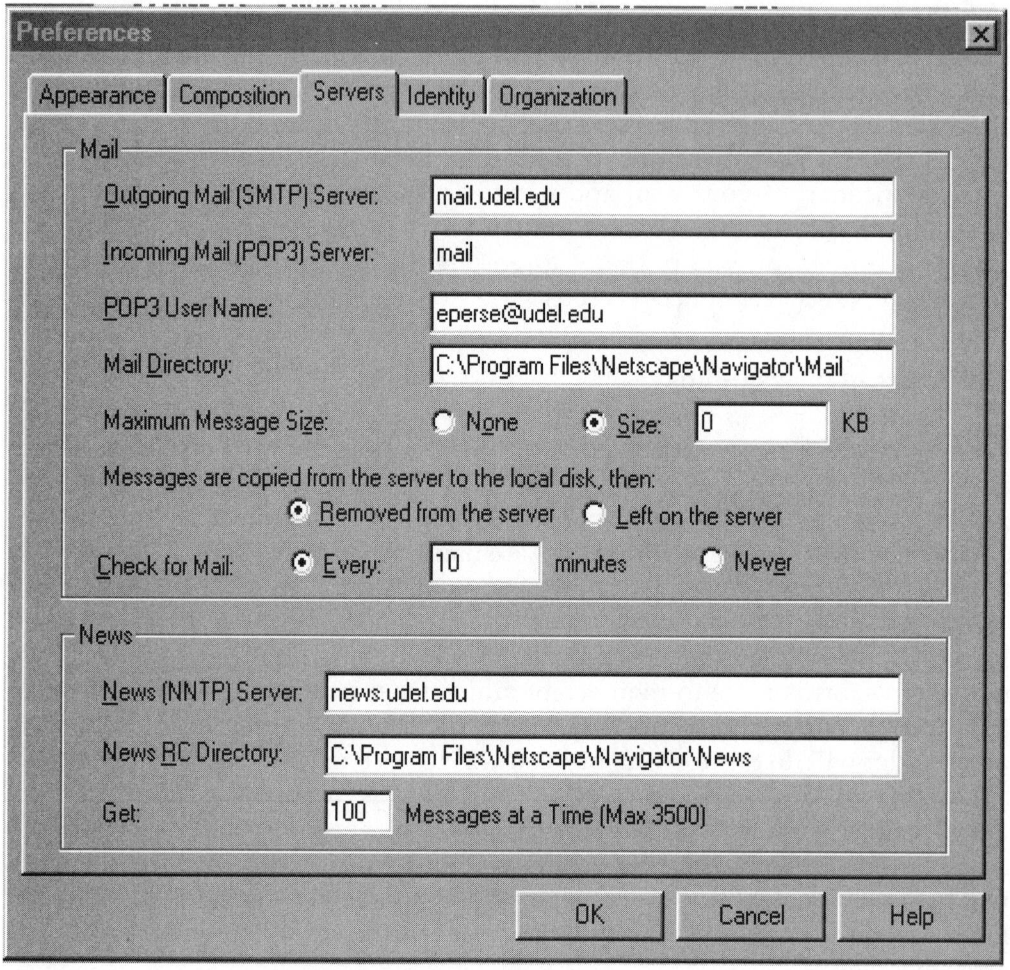

Figure 4.3 (Copyright © 1996 Netscape Communications Corp. Used with permission. All rights reserved. This electronic file or page may not be reprinted or copied without the express written permission of Netscape.)

the user wants to subscribe to each one. This can result in many screens of names of newsgroups being pushed at the user. Most of those new newsgroups will have little interest, and looking at each one individually can take up a good deal of time. Fortunately, trn includes an "N" command to signal that the user is not interested in subscribing to any of the new newsgroups and screens of new newsgroups will then fly by.

It is much more efficient to use the Get command on mainframes to access a specific newsgroup, if you know the exact name. If you do not know the right name, use the Search command to get a list of newsgroups whose titles contain certain strings of words. Then, use the Get command to bring these postings to your terminal.

Note: Although most Usenet newsgroups are widely available, not all servers or services have access to every newsgroup. Many newsgroups that discuss sensitive topics (like drugs or sex) are frequently blocked to prevent access by those who might be offended by those discussions.

Reading and Subscribing. Once you have located a newsgroup on a topic that interests you, you will want to use your newsreader to read the postings. Some specialized newsgroups have a manageable number of recent postings. Other more active newsgroups, though, may have hundreds or even thousands of postings. How can you separate the wheat from the chaff? Fortunately, newsgroups offer two ways for you to sift through postings. First, newsgroup postings are organized into **threads**, or collections of postings about a similar topic. If you are interested in the topic, follow the thread. If you are not, delete or ignore the entire thread. Second, most considerate users will include a subject header describing the content of the posting. (Most newsreaders will not send a message off without a subject heading.) So, if you don't want to take the time to read every posting, you can scan the subjects and read only those that interest you. Figure 4.4 (p. 78) shows Netscape News. You can see how messages are "nested" into subject-related threads.

Reading newsgroup postings is easy. All newsreaders deliver the articles in a directory form (organized by threads). Simply move your cursor to the article or thread that you want to read and hit the enter key (if you are on a mainframe computer). If you are using a Windows- or Mac-based newsreader, double-click on the message to read it.

You can read the postings in a newsgroup without subscribing, but you might find it easier to subscribe to newsgroups that you read regularly. Subscribing has several advantages: first, subscribing is like having a bookmark to a newsgroup. Whenever you open your newsreader program, it remembers the newsgroups you have subscribed to and goes to the server and retrieves the messages automatically. Moreover, the newsreader remembers which articles, or postings, you've read, so it only delivers new postings. This saves you going through screens of material that you may have already read.

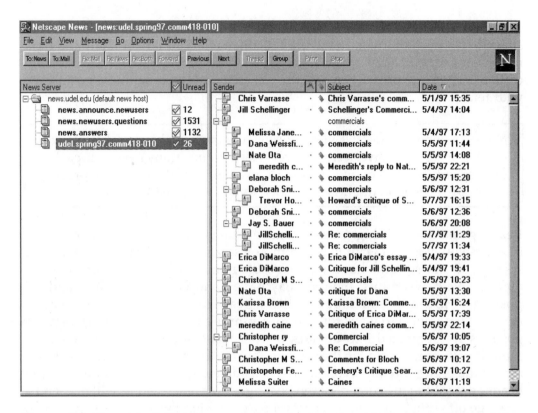

Figure 4.4 (Copyright © 1996 Netscape Communications Corp. Used with permission. All rights reserved. This electronic file or page may not be reprinted or copied without the express written permission of Netscape.)

As a result, subscribing is a good idea and easy to do. Simply find the Subscribe command at the bottom of your newsreader screen, if you are on a mainframe computer. On Windows-based newsreaders, subscribing is as easy as clicking on a menu item or next to the name of the newsgroup. Remember, if you should find the newsgroup less useful or less interesting sometime in the future, unsubscribing is just as easy as subscribing.

Once you have read a posting, you have several options. Most of the time, simply reading the posting is enough. With most newsreaders, once you have read a posting, it is marked "read," and you never see that posting again. Hence, there is no need to delete or remove specific postings. If you would like to keep postings available to be read again, find the option to change the "read/unread" status. It might be easier, however, to save or print specific postings that interest you. Lurking, or keeping up with newsgroups yet never contributing can be fun, but it might be more enjoyable to join in the discussions yourself. Next we will discuss different responses to newsgroup postings.

Saving. Most often, simply reading a posting is all you will need to do. There may be information in a posting, however, that is valuable enough that you want to be able to access it again. Some newsgroups archive their postings, but not all do. So you may want either a hard or electronic copy of the posting. Printing is easy in any newsreader. Simply click on the printer icon or execute the Print command.

You can also save a posting to a file. On mainframe systems, find the Save command at the bottom of the screen and follow the directions. On Windows-based newsreaders like Netscape, simply use the Save As option in the File menu.

Replying. After reading a newsgroup posting, you may find that you want to add something to the discussion. For example, you have been reading about the Communication Decency Act on the newsgroup your instructor has set up for class discussion. You realize that one of the postings reports some incorrect information. You have three options to communicate what you know: You can reply directly to the author to allow him or her to correct the mistake, post a "follow-up" message to the newsgroup to correct the error publicly, or do both.

On mainframe systems you would contact the author and the newsgroup one at a time. To reply to the author of a posting, highlight the posting in the newsreader and enter the command for "Reply." You will probably be placed in one of the mainframe editors. Enter your message, and execute the Send command. This message will then be sent privately to the author of the article.

If you also want to send a message to the newsgroup, you need to send a "follow-up" message. To post a follow-up message, execute the Follow-up command. Usually the previous message will be included, but check to see whether there is a separate command to insert the message. Edit it, if you wish, and enter your own message. Then, execute the Send command. Once the follow-up is sent, it will be posted as a new article in the same thread as the earlier posting, available for everyone to read.

Replying is much easier with Netscape News. Look at the toolbar bar or under the Message menu. There are menu items and buttons to Post Reply (which sends the message to the newsgroup), Mail Reply (which sends mail to the author of the posting), and Post and Mail Reply (which does both at the same time). Click on the menu item or button that you want, enter and edit your message, and send. It's just that simple!

Warning! Not all newsgroups allow just anyone to post messages. Some newsgroups are moderated. That means that someone screens the messages and controls which ones are posted on the server. Moderated newsgroups usually have more focused discussions.

Forwarding. There may be times when you believe a particular newsgroup posting would be of interest to your friends or classmates. On such occasions, forwarding a posting to a third party is similar to forwarding e-mail. On mainframe systems, find the Forward or Mail command at the bottom of the screen. Some newsreaders may ask if you want to mail only the article or the entire thread. Fill in the information as you are prompted, including the e-mail address of the intended recipient, and send. Remember that you have the choice to quit anytime if you change your mind. The Quit command will also be listed at the bottom of your screen.

In Netscape News, click on the Forward button or choose "Forward" in the Message menu. Type in the address of the intended recipient, edit the posting if you wish, and click on Send.

Posting. Of course, you can initiate a new thread by posting an article on an entirely new subject. Before you do, however, make sure that you are familiar with the topics and rules of the group. Check out the **FAQs** (frequently asked questions) to make sure you're not initiating a topic that's already been discussed to death. You should also check out the news.announce.newsusers newsgroup that includes information for new users. This newsgroup includes documents to give new users background about Usenet and "netiquette," as well as FAQs about newsgroups in general. Once you have done a little research, you're ready to jump into the discussion.

On mainframe systems, execute the command to post an article to a newsgroup. Many systems use Pnews, a program for posting to newsgroups. That command might activate one of the mainframe editors. On some systems, though, you might have to make a file for your posting before you begin this process. Try your system out to see how you need to proceed. Once you execute the Post command, you will probably be asked to type answers to a series of questions, including the name of the newsgroup and the subject. Make sure that you type the name of the newsgroup correctly. Just as with e-mail, a simple typing error will make your posting undeliverable. Chose your subject carefully. Make sure it is simple enough to understand yet interesting enough to grab the attention of the group's readers. You may also be asked other information specific to your system. Once you have answered the queries, execute the Send command.

As you might have guessed by now, this process is much simpler using a Window- or Mac-based newsreader. Simply highlight the newsgroup to which you want to post, click on the To: News button or the New News Message item under the File menu. Type your message, include any attachments, and click Send.

Just like that, you're communicating online!

Some Hints on Newsgroup Writing Style

- Keep your messages short and to the point. Write no more than you need to to make your point. Most postings should be only a few sentences, and even the most complex postings should be no longer than a few paragraphs.

- Be concise without being cryptic. Remember that the Internet is an international medium. Don't use "cute" phrases or spellings; readers from other countries may not understand them. Don't eliminate articles (for example, "the") or other function words, because this may make your posting difficult to read or understand.

- Learn to use widely-understood emoticons (see p. 18) and shorthand abbreviations. Some of the most common abbreviations used in newsgroup postings are: IMO (in my opinion), IMHO (in my humble opinion), LOL (laughing out loud), BTW (by the way), and BBFN (bye bye for now). You will pick up others as you read and post.

LISTSERV AND NEWSGROUP ETIQUETTE

- **Lurk** before you leap! Don't enter a discussion until you've become acquainted with the topics and the rules. Contributing redundant messages may be considered rude and is certainly a waste of time for the group members.

- Check out the group's FAQs (frequently asked questions). These will give you background information about the group, including answers to questions that are asked so often that the group doesn't want to waste time reposting the answers.

- Do not use listservs or newsgroups for personal messages. Don't send messages intended for only one person to the entire list. If you ask for information from list members, request that they send the information directly to you, rather than sending it to the entire group. If your topic is of general interest to the group, post a summary of the responses you have received. Do not expect privacy. Your messages and postings can be easily forwarded to others. And many groups archive their group's activity. Therefore, any embarrassing or damaging messages could be around for a long time.

• Don't expect group members to do your research for you. Most members of a group will ignore or react unfavorably to requests for general information that is readily available. This is especially true when students post to an academic newsgroup or listserv and request help with a project or paper (such as trying to get a list of references). Almost invariably, that student will be directed (sometimes quite harshly) to visit their library.

• Request help only for specialized topics. And remember, any information is only as good as its source. Evaluate anything that you learn from listservs or newsgroups carefully before you act on it!

• Never type in all CAPITALS! This is called "shouting" and considered rude.

• Be tolerant of mistakes in others' spelling, typing, and grammar. Although we should always be careful about mechanics in everything that we write, it is difficult to make corrections in some news systems. Let mistakes pass. To comment or **flame** someone because of mechanical errors is rude, a waste of others' time, and diverts the discussion from the topic at hand.

• If anyone should flame you, ignore it. Don't take flames seriously. If you enjoy flaming, send your messages to others who appreciate it: alt.flame.hall-of-flame.

• Don't **troll**, or post messages designed to agitate the group. A newsgroup for vegetarians is not the place to post recipes for armadillo chili!

• Keep your posts short and to the point. Don't go off on tangents. Keep focused on the thread of the discussion. Quote only those parts of the message to which you are referring.

• Learn to recognize emoticons and shorthand symbols.

- Use descriptive subject headings so that other readers will be able to screen your postings easily.

- Listservs and newsgroups are not popularity contests. Don't send messages only to announce your agreement with a previous message. "Dittos" waste time and resources.

- Avoid elaborate signature files. They can be distracting and use up Internet resources and disk storage.

- Never spam—even if you are sure that the group is interested in the product or service that you are selling. They aren't! When newsgroups become clogged with advertising posts, readers abandon them and the newsgroups then lose their ability to conduct public discussion. Some readers actually retaliate against inappropriate advertising by forwarding lots of messages back to the offender, thus using up their e-mail resources. Most users, however, just ignore the offense and leave the newsgroup.

- We advise you to always identify yourself whenever you communicate— even on the Internet. If you believe that revealing your true identity could lead you to be harassed (remember that your e-mail address becomes part of the message), consider using an anonymous remailer. These remailers, however, should not be used frivolously. Remember, information is only as good as its source and anonymous information cannot be accurately evaluated.

CHAPTER 5

Transferring Files Using FTP

Although on several occasions we have hesitated to forecast the direction of some rapidly changing Internet technology, there is one prediction we will make with great confidence: the longer you work on and the more proficient you become with the Internet, the more you will encounter the need to transfer files from one computer to another. Whether sharing information with a coworker, downloading the latest shareware program, or making duplicate copies of important files, you will find the use of **file transfer protocol** (FTP) to transport files over the Internet an indispensable tool.

In Chapter 1 we organized the discussion of FTP under two headings: communicating and accessing information. In this chapter, we will alter our organization a bit and address two questions about transferring files with FTP: Why and how? We will also introduce a third topic, archiving files.

Under the second question (how?) we will discuss several different approaches to using FTP. Which one works best for you will depend on the computer you use and the software you have at your disposal. We will also tell you how to obtain additional software for FTP, because we think you're definitely going to need it. Finally, we will conclude in our usual way, with a brief discussion of the ethics involved in transferring files across the Internet.

WHY TRANSFER FILES?

We believe there are three primary reasons that Internet users transfer files between computers, although you (and we) could probably think of dozens of additional, "lesser" ones. We will present the three primary reasons in order from the "most likely" to "least likely" reason for transferring files.

Anonymous FTP

We introduced the topic of anonymous FTP in Chapter 1 under the heading of accessing information, so let us briefly review those comments. Recall that anonymous FTP takes place in an unsecured environment in which the server does not require a log on ID or password to connect to the client software. Instead, you log on to the server using the ID "anonymous" (literally, by typing "anonymous"), and are usually required to supply your e-mail address as the password.

This type of client/server relationship is most often established when the organization that owns the server wants the general public to have access to the files that reside on the server computer. Generally, this public access is restricted to no more than a few directories rather than the entire computer, thus providing a combination of openness and security on the same machine.

What type of files actually reside on the server depends almost totally on the type of organization that owns or controls it. Our experience suggests that you will most frequently encounter computer software (shareware) that is available for downloading on a trial basis, with payment due later if you continue to use the software. Later in this chapter we will suggest some Web locations where you can acquire shareware (or better yet, freeware) for use as either an FTP client or server.

A second, common use of anonymous FTP is to acquire upgrades or "fixes" for commercial software that you already own. Microsoft Corporation, for example, has provided numerous small additions to its Windows 95 software, some to rectify problems and others to enhance the original programs. A similar add-on from Microsoft is an extension to their word-processing software, Word for Windows. By downloading and installing an upgrade called "Internet Assistant," a user can easily and directly convert Word documents to HTML files that can be posted and read on the WWW.

Of course, numerous other types of information that be posted on an FTP server—almost as many as your imagination can conjure up. This is especially true in an academic environment, where an instructor might make available handouts, study guides, lecture notes, previous versions of exams, and so forth. In fact, almost any type of material that instructors traditionally pass out in class now make excellent candidates for posting on a server.

Hardly a week goes by that one of the two authors of this book doesn't post something on the Internet for a class. Frankly, our preference is to post such academic material on a Web server rather than one devoted to FTP, but that is merely a preference that reflects our university's computing environment. If your instructor has asked you to buy this book for class, chances are that you have already begun acquiring class information from an Internet server.

Sharing Files

Let us begin by voicing a criticism of contemporary higher education in America: students spend far too much time working alone and not enough time working in groups. We label this a criticism, because the tendency in the professional world you will shortly enter is just the opposite. Real work in the "real world" is most often done by committees, task forces, project groups, work teams, and the like. The exact label for these groups is not important. What is salient is that you will almost certainly spend a lot of your professional time working on projects with other people.

This, of course, implies communication and sharing—sharing ideas, information, and creative talent, as well as sharing the computer resources necessary to support those ideas and talent. We can envision three distinct ways that this computer sharing is usually accomplished, only one of which is via FTP.

Perhaps the most obvious approach is that you can share files with coworkers by attaching them to your e-mail messages. We have discussed this approach at some length in previous chapters because we believe it works quite well. There are, however, two shortcomings to this approach that must be considered. First, everyone must have the e-mail software necessary to send and receive attachments quickly and easily. Colleagues who have only a mainframe e-mail program (Pine Mail, for example) find dealing with attachments cumbersome and inefficient.

The second potential drawback is that e-mail attachments flow in only one direction and, thus, are under the total control of the person on whose computer they reside. We describe this as a "potential" problem because there are certainly times when working in this manner is quite acceptable. On the other hand, if there are documents or material that the entire work group requires to complete its task, this unidirectional flow of information will probably create more problems than it solves.

Another approach to sharing information with coworkers involves working on a local area network (LAN). If all of your computers are linked together on departmental network, the files that need to be shared can be located on a central computer (again, called a server), and each team member can be given access. We fully realize, however, that students almost never have access to this type of networking, so we mention it only for the sake of completeness. Subsequently, when you begin working in a professional environment, your likelihood of encountering a LAN will become much higher, and you will find this approach to be a very satisfactory way to share information.

Finally, we consider the FTP approach. Although the Internet is clearly not a "local" network, it is a network nonetheless. As a result, it is possible to designate a computer as a server and allow your team members to have access to the files on that computer. If you use this type of arrangement, you would be wise to issue IDs and passwords to each team member, thus creating a secure client/ server relationship.

You could make the argument that nobody outside of your group would really want to copy files and documents from a bunch of college students, and we might agree. Still, now is the time to develop good work habits. Learning how to establish and use a secure FTP will not only be useful later in your professional life, it may even be one of those small advantages that actually lands you your first job. Nothing like a little added incentive, eh?

Tip: The more you use the Internet, the more you will encounter sites that require a password. If you try to devise a unique password for every site, you will quickly forget most of them, thus causing serious frustration the next time you try to log on.

Accordingly, we recommend establishing only two passwords: a public and a private one. The public password is the one you use at Internet sites, FTP servers, shared files on LAN's, and so forth. If it is discovered by a would-be hacker, the damage that person can do is, thus, kept to a minimum.

In contrast, use your "private" password to protect personal and potentially valuable material, such as your account on your university's computer, or perhaps especially private files on your personal computer.

This should not be taken to mean that we don't recommend changing these two passwords. We do, often! Nevertheless, using only two passwords will not only solve the memory problem but will also greatly decrease the probability that others might snoop about in files you want to keep confidential.

We will conclude this section by mentioning a fourth way of sharing information with your colleagues: the old fashioned way. You can obviously pass around diskettes or even printed copies of your documents. BORING! But more than boring, what useful experience do you gain that you can take with you after college? The answer: None!

Remember that the premise of this book is that a reasonable proficiency with the Internet and its various functions is a prerequisite to a successful career as a communication professional. Taking shortcuts now will cost you dearly later! We know that you've heard this before, probably from one or both of your parents. But they were right and so are we. Enough said.

Archiving Files

We began this chapter with a fearless prediction; let us offer another. Sooner or later you will lose an important file. Whether you mistakenly delete it, save another file with the same name, or it just disappears due to the magic of computer gremlins, one of these days you will have that sinking feeling in the pit of your stomach when you realize that all of your hard work has just been vaporized.

Under other circumstances, we might be tempted to launch into a brief sermon about the virtues of backing up your work onto floppies, tape, or another suitable medium. We will ignore this temptation, however, because our experience suggests that this advice won't work. Until you personally lose a significant amount of time and effort because you failed to have a backup copy of your files, nothing we write here will register. However, after you have experienced disaster firsthand, there will be no need for us to say anything. You too will be among the converted.

In any case, our purpose in this section is to talk about a close relative of backing up, namely, archiving your work. Archiving, of course, is the answer to the question: What do I do with all of those files that I'm not currently using but don't want to discard? You could, no doubt, put them onto floppy disks, but then what do you do with all of those disks, other than lose them?

Let's think seriously, then, about using FTP to store those valuable but not current files by transferring them to another computer. We are aware that many college students don't have even one computer, let alone two, but bear with us. Most students have access to a PC or a Mac, and most of these students have a student account on one of their university's mainframe computers. This is all you need to begin a successful program of archiving your files. If you are fortunate enough to have your own computer, then you have even more reason to think about archiving.

We begin with the question: Why archive? Many times, the files on your personal computer have served their current purpose, but are still too valuable to discard. Perhaps they contain material you might use again; perhaps they contain formatting or other design elements that might come in handy in the future; or perhaps you need the space on your computer's hard disk for your current work.

The solution to any of these dilemmas is to FTP these files from your computer to your account on the university mainframe. We recommend that you archive these files to directories on the mainframe with the same names as those on your personal computer. This avoids confusion when you want to find these files in the future.

> **Tip:** Although space limitations do not allow us to elaborate, we also recommend that you compress these files into a single "zipped" file before transferring them. If you are unfamiliar with the concept of file compression and the "zip" format, see someone in your computer center about how to do this. You could also do a Web search to learn the basics. It's easy and it saves massive amounts of disk space.

The advantages of archiving in this manner are several and mostly obvious. First, you've retained those potentially useful files. Second, you've made additional space on your computer's hard disk. And third, none of this has cost you anything. Talk about an impressive cost/benefit ratio!

We might also add a fourth advantage: Even if you are not yet in the habit of backing up regularly, we assure you that the folks at your university's computer center certainly are. As computer professionals, they are well aware of the costs (both financial and otherwise) of having an entire mainframe crash and losing all of its data. As a result, they back up everything daily.

The benefit to you is that your files will always be there. Which brings us to our last suggestion. Considering that having someone else back things up for you nightly is such a wonderful safeguard, why not take advantage of it for current projects? As you're working on that research paper, or that major presentation, or something important like your resume, why not FTP it to your mainframe account for safekeeping? As before, it's easy and it's free.

You can be assured that every chapter of this book was placed safely on our university's computer the moment it was finished and sometimes when it was only partially completed. We have lost plenty of files to those computer gremlins. Accordingly, we believe that being slightly paranoid about the safety of our files is not an illness, but rather a survival instinct.

HOW TO TRANSFER FILES

The software that is required to connect to and transfer files between two computers is either client software or server software. In this section, we will talk only about the programs necessary to turn your computer into an FTP client. Later in this chapter, we will briefly describe where you can obtain programs to make your computer a server.

We have chosen to divide the many programs that perform FTP into two basic categories: (1) those that employ a "graphical interface" such as those in Windows-based PCs or Macs, and (2) FTP programs whose commands are typed on a command line as found on UNIX mainframes. We will discuss the former more than the latter, suggesting that you should endeavor to avoid command-line FTP whenever possible.

Graphical FTP

The concept of the graphical interface has been displayed by many of the programs we have shown you in figures from previous chapters. This is especially true of Netscape (and also Internet Explorer), which is the ultimate in graphical approaches to the Internet. The same concepts of "point and click" (and a new one, "drag") characterize how you go about transferring files using these programs. Within this broad category, however, the are three different approaches to implementing file transfer, so we will discuss them separately.

Web Browsers. One of the simplest ways to acquire files via FTP is directly through your trusty Web browser. Recall from Chapter 3 (p. 37) that one of the "protocols" recognized by Netscape (and all other browsers as well) is the FTP protocol. After you inform Netscape, for example, that you want to go to an FTP server, the browser does the rest.

We will illustrate this simplicity by going to a prominent FTP site on the Internet, the server for the Microsoft Corporation. The URL that we must enter for this site is: ftp://ftp.microsoft.com/. The result of entering this URL in the Location box (and pressing Enter!) is displayed in Figure 5.1. Admittedly, the screen in Figure 5.1 doesn't look very "graphical," but compare it to the command-line approach!

Because this is the main level of the Microsoft site, numerous directories lie beneath it; these are symbolized by "folders." Clicking on one of them will take you directly to the files in that directory. In contrast, individual files of various

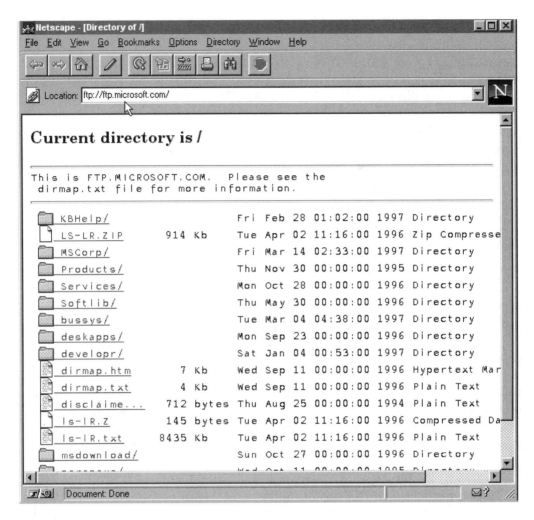

Figure 5.1 (Copyright © 1996 Netscape Communications Corp. Used with permission. All rights reserved. This electronic file or page may not be reprinted or copiedwithout the express writtten permission of Netscape.)

types are displayed by symbols that represent sheets of paper. You will begin to recognize these icons rather quickly because they are almost universal among programs that use the graphical approach to FTP.

To transfer a file to your computer, simply click on that file. Netscape will produce a dialogue box that will ask you where on your computer you wish to save the file. Select the appropriate folder, click on Save, and the transfer will begin. Depending on the size of the file, the actual transfer may take anywhere from several to many (30+) minutes. Just grab a cup of coffee, or play a computer game, or do some other work. When the transfer is complete, Netscape will return to normal, thus allowing you to browse or FTP some more.

Tip: We believe it is a good idea to establish a single directory or folder to serve as the sole location for files that are transferred to your computer. We call ours the "Download" directory, but the name is irrelevant. Using a single directory places all downloaded files in one location, either for installing or deleting. In contrast, scattering them around your hard disk is a good way to lose track of them completely.

Given how easy this seems, you're probably thinking there must be a drawback. Of course, you're right. The primary shortcoming of using a Web browser to transfer files is that the direction of transfer is one-way, from the server to your computer. There is no mechanism for you to transfer files in the other direction.

This limitation does not pose a problem for many types of transfers, though, especially those involving anonymous FTP. The primary goal of such a transfer is to obtain a file or a program from another computer and transfer it to your own. Because a Web browser automates the entire process, such transfers are especially easy. On the other hand, when sharing files with others or archiving your files for safekeeping is the goal, software that allows bidirectional transfer is required. Accordingly, we now turn our attention to programs of this type.

Dedicated FTP Clients. Many programs are available whose sole purpose is to serve as a bidirectional FTP client. Some of these are reasonably inexpensive commercial programs (less than $50), others are shareware programs, and a few quite excellent programs are actually given away as freeware. As with most things in life, you tend to get what you pay for, so the commercial programs have additional features, especially when compared to the free ones. Nevertheless, if you are just beginning your experience with file transfers, the freeware programs will do most admirably, and we'll show you how to acquire them a bit later in this chapter.

To illustrate the difference between these dedicated clients and a Web browser, we have chosen an excellent yet reasonably priced commercial program called, WS_FTP95 Pro. Figure 5.2 displays an image of this client again logged on to the Microsoft FTP site.

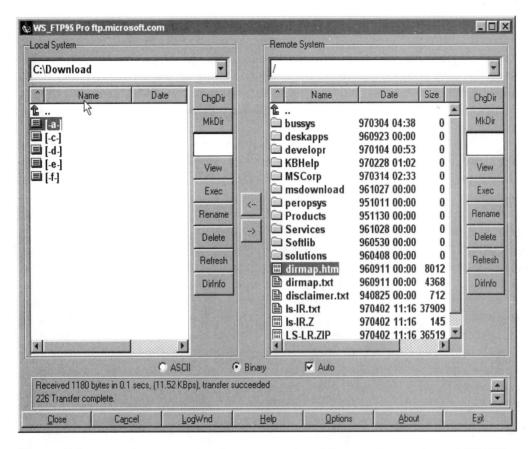

Figure 5.2 (Screen shot reprinted with permission from Microsoft Corporation and WS-FTP Professional by Ipswitch, Inc.)

Several differences between this software and Netscape are immediately apparent. First, notice that two windows are visible, one containing the files at the Microsoft site and one displaying the contents of the "Download" directory on the client computer. Currently, there are no files in that directory.

Note also the various "buttons" for viewing, executing, and renaming the various files and directories in either site. Because this is a commercial site operated by Microsoft, the server will not allow us to carry out some of these commands, for example, renaming files on their site. Similarly, the server would prohibit us from transferring files to Microsoft. This prohibition, however, is imposed solely by the server and for obvious reasons. The client software is quite capable of transferring in either direction.

Finally, near the bottom of this figure you can see three check boxes labeled "ASCII," "Binary," and "Auto." Binary and ASCII represent the two types of files you would normally transfer. Recall that binary files contain computer codes (for example, image files, word-processed files, or actual working programs), while ASCII files contain only text with little or no formatting. These two types of files are transferred differently, and the client must tell the server which type of transfer is desired.

In Netscape, this decision was automatic and completely hidden; the browser made the decision without asking. Similarly, in WS_FTP95 Pro, we can check the Auto button and the program will carry out a similar type of automatic decision-making process. The difference is that in WS_FTP95 Pro we have the option to make that decision manually. When we eventually introduce a command-line client, you will have no choice whatsoever: you must make an explicit decision about ASCII versus binary with each and every transfer.

With software similar to that in Figure 5.2, transfers are carried out in one of two ways. First, you select the file you wish to transfer by clicking on it once. Then you either (1) click on the button with the arrow in the middle column that points toward your computer, or (2) simply click and drag the file into your computer's window. A dialogue box will appear, you click OK, and the transfer begins. To transfer files from your client computer to the server (if allowed), you need only reverse the process. Click on the arrow pointing towards the server, or click and drag the file into the server's window. As before, the amount of time the transfer actually consumes will be dependent on the size of the file.

Unlike a Web browser, a dedicated FTP client such as the one in Figure 5.2 allows for great flexibility in setting various options that control the transfer. You can define the actions for most of the "buttons," decide what directory automatically appears in the left-hand window, or what files types are treated as binary as opposed to ASCII. These options are so numerous that we can't go into any more detail here. Suffice it to say that the ability to customize almost all of the characteristics regarding how you transfer your files is one of the features you pay for when you purchase commercial software.

Specialized Programs. To fully complete our discussion of various graphical approaches to file transfer, we need to include a few paragraphs about truly "high-end" commercial programs. These are relatively expensive programs (usually costing more than $100) and are designed to transfer files and offer remote control capabilities over several different media—for example, cables, modems, the Internet, and even through infrared hookups.

We are referring to programs with names such as "Carbon Copy," "Close Up," "Rapid Remote," and the one we will illustrate here, "Laplink." Many of these programs were originally designed to facilitate the transfer of files between a person's laptop computer and their main computer, usually a "desktop" computer. This allowed people who used a laptop in their travels (or to take notes in class) to synchronize the files and programs between their two computers. In their original versions, file transfers were done almost exclusively through a special cable that linked the two computers through their printer ports.

With the advent of the Internet, however, these programs greatly expanded their ability to transfer files to other media. By having one copy of the program running on the desktop computer and another on the laptop, users can now transfer files over the Internet in a manner very similar to the FTP approaches we have been describing. Not surprisingly, however, the cost of this type of software also ensures that it will contain many special features and additional options.

A sample transfer session using the Laplink program is displayed in Figure 5.3 (p. 96). In this example, the transfer is between Courtright's home computer and the PC at his office. This figure looks similar to the WS_FTP95 Pro program displayed in Figure 5.2 (p. 93), with two notable exceptions: Although there are two windows, one for the client and one for the server (interestingly, these programs frequently refer to the two computers as "host" and "remote"), there are also two smaller windows for each computer. Higher-level directories or drives are located in the left window, and lower-level directories or files are found on the right. This separation provides these programs with an advantage over many "low-end" FTP clients—namely, they allow for the transfer of entire directories, as well as individual files.

Beyond these two enhancements (the ability to transfer over several media and the ability to transfer entire folders), these programs operate conceptually the same as transfers using FTP. OK, so why buy one? If your only purpose is to transfer files over the Internet, there is no good reason; inexpensive or free client software will meet your needs just as well. Even more important, these programs only transfer files between two copies of themselves, thus making them useless for anonymous FTP. Again, a basic FTP client will prove superior.

If, on the other hand, you own a laptop that you need to keep in sync with your desktop computer, one of these programs will pay for itself many times over. Or if you make numerous transfers between the same two computers (say, your home computer and a computer at the office), these programs offer numerous "bells and whistles" that could justify their cost. As a student, of course,

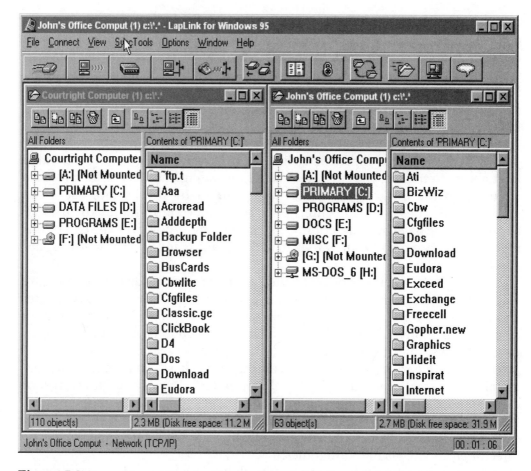

Figure 5.3 (Screen shot reprinted with permission from Microsoft Corporation and Traveling Software, Inc.)

money is usually pretty scarce, so this advice may actually be for later in your career as a communication professional. That's fine, because we predict that in the future there will be much more emphasis on file transfers of all types.

Command Line FTP (Use it Only When You Have to!)

Now that we have touted the utility and efficiency of these various graphical approaches to FTP, we step back in time to discuss the original and most basic (primitive) approach to transferring files: typing commands on the command line. In this approach, nothing is automatic. All of the functions and options that were implemented automatically by the graphical programs must now be explicitly typed in by the user.

This approach to FTP is frequently found on UNIX mainframe computers, as well as computers that use the PC-DOS operating system. There are no graphics and it is completely text-based. Figure 5.4 (p. 98) shows how the Microsoft site would look if you logged on through a command-line FTP program. The screen is black, the characters are white, and the command line is the last line on the screen. Ugly! The screen contains the results of a "dir" command, which asks the computer to display the contents of the current directory.

To use this approach, you will have to know more than 30 separate commands to control your FTP session. Some of these commands are obvious, such as "bye" or "help." Others tend to be a bit more mysterious, such as, "hash," "mget," "bput," and "ls." There is a help command that provides some assistance, but we would argue that it is as primitive as the rest of the approach.

We will not present any detail on these numerous commands, because our primary recommendation is that you use this approach to transferring files "only when you have to." It stinks! And anyone who would recommend it over the more modern, graphical approaches is either crazy or a fool. (Do you think we feel strongly about this?) Nevertheless, there are a few instances when you simply cannot avoid the command-line approach if you wish to transfer a file.

When Do You Have to? One instance when the command-line approach is unavoidable is when you are using a mainframe, UNIX account instead of a PC or a Mac to transfer files. Such mainframe computers have little or no graphical capabilities, so the command-line, text-based approach is all that is available. If you find yourself in this situation, we urge you to consult a manual at your computer center for the necessary commands or, better yet, find a friendly consultant who will walk you through the process. If you're adventuresome, you could try to go it alone, but be prepared for a very long session.

A second situation that might require command-line FTP is when you are initially setting up your PC or Mac and do not yet have any graphical software installed. For example, how do you obtain a graphical client from an FTP site if you don't already have a graphical client? The answer, of course, is through command-line FTP. In a thoughtful move, Microsoft chose to provide a command-line FTP client with Windows 95 (that is what you see in Figure 5.4). If you don't have such a program, then you must resort to using a friend's computer and transporting everything via floppy disks: a form of "file transfer," to be sure, but not the type we want to encourage.

Figure 5.4 (Screen shot reprinted with permission from Microsoft Corporation.)

> **Tip:** Sooner or later you will find—no matter how painful it may be—that you need to use this command-line approach. Most often, this will be during a minor emergency where other alternatives have failed. This is not the type of situation in which you should confront command-line FTP for the first time. Practice in advance. Get the necessary manuals or personal assistance. If you wait, you'll be in for a major ordeal!

Other than the two scenarios we just described, our advice is to concentrate on graphical approaches to FTP. To encourage you in this direction, we will now suggest where to find both clients and servers to help you transfer your files.

OBTAINING CLIENTS AND SERVERS

There are numerous places on the Internet where you can acquire not only FTP software, but also shareware and freeware of all types. In the interest of brevity, we will present only a single site as part of our discussion. No doubt you could find quite a few more by using your Web browser to search for terms such as "shareware," "freeware," or "software."

A site that we find particularly useful is: http://www.tucows.com/. Why is it called "tucows"? Because it contains "<u>T</u>he <u>U</u>ltimate <u>C</u>ollection <u>O</u>f <u>W</u>insock <u>S</u>oftware." Besides offering a wide array of software for the Internet, this site describes each selection and rates the quality of each program from 1 to 5. Instead of using a number system or even stars to rate a program, however, this site provides a "cow" rating (five cows are best). This bovine theme is a bit unique, but the software selection is truly outstanding.

Evidently, many others agree with our opinion that this is a sensational Web site, because it is so busy that the purpose of the main page at the above URL is only to direct you to an affiliate site where you can actually acquire the software. Well over two dozen sites are listed, so the best option is to pick the one geographically closest to you, thus decreasing the time that a transfer will take.

Since the sites are all the same, we selected one at random. The result was the URL: http://tucows.phoenix.net/window95.html. Figure 5.5 (p. 100) displays the listings of various types of software that are found at this site. Note that there are categories for virtually every type of Internet software. Go ahead and explore! If you're into the Internet, this is like being a kid in a candy shop.

Our purpose here, however, is to discuss possible FTP clients that you might acquire. By clicking on the listing for "FTP, " you will go to another URL that presents and evaluates numerous FTP clients. We urge you to go through them all, but here we will present only one.

We have opted to recommend an FTP client that has two advantages: (1) it has numerous features to assist you with your transfers, and (2) it is free. This client is shown in Figure 5.6 (p. 101). You might recognize the name for this program: WS_FTP95 LE. This is the freeware version of the software we discussed earlier. The designation "LE" stands for "light edition," meaning that it is not quite as full-featured as the commercial "Pro" version we saw before. Nevertheless, the fact that it is free more than makes up for the few features it is lacking. We suggest that you download it and see for yourself. Remember, you can always go back for another client if you find this one not to your liking.

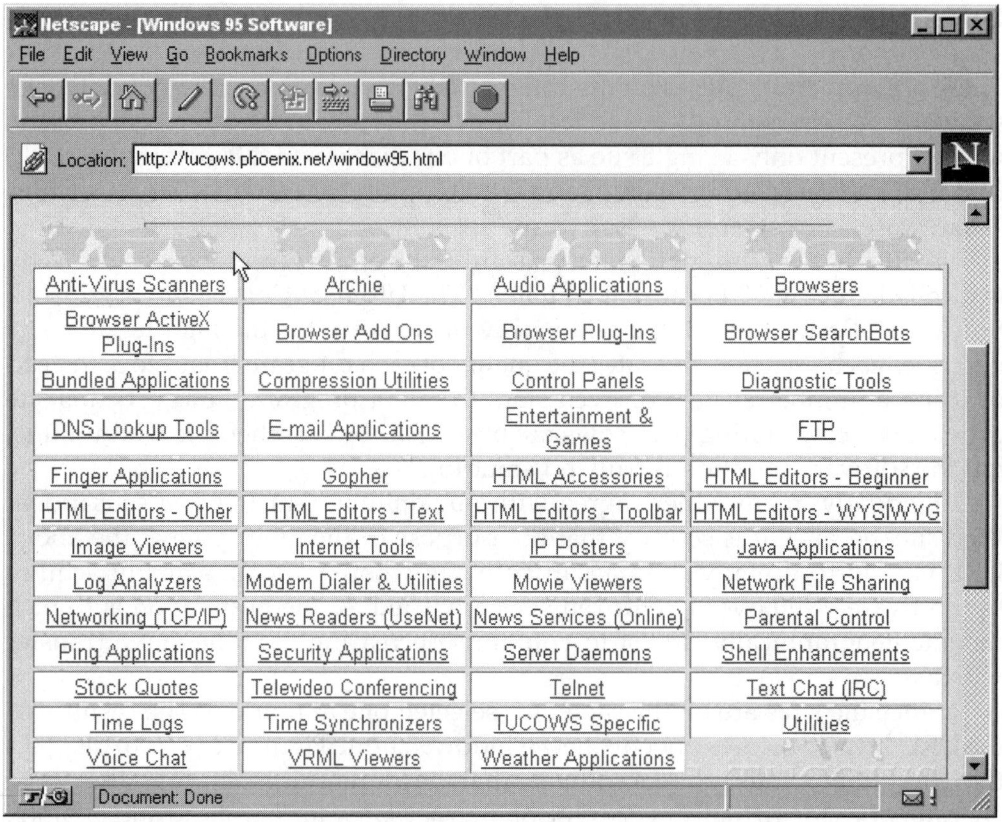

Figure 5.5 (Screen shot reprinted with permission from Microsoft Corporation and Tucows International, Inc.)

This client, however, constitutes only half of the two pieces of software we recommend that you acquire. The other, of course, is an FTP server, thus allowing you to turn your personal computer into a server and allow others (or yourself) to access it over the Internet.

> **Note:** In this description, we have only discussed the PC version of FTP clients. Although tucows has an entire section devoted to Mac software, we don't use Macs and thus we have no personal experience that would allow us to recommend one program over another. The procedures for acquiring Mac software, however, are the same, but those of you who are Mac users will have to do a bit more trial and error to find the program you prefer.

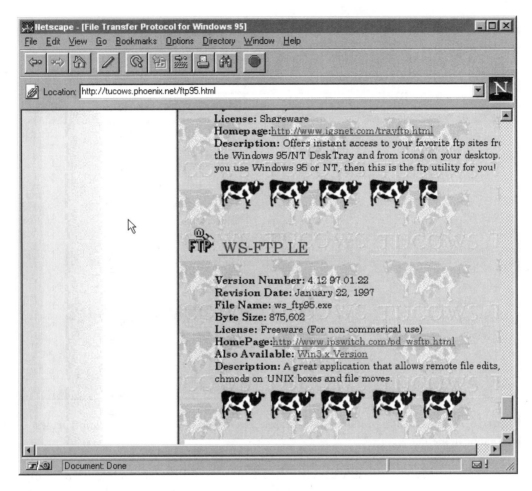

Figure 5.6 (Screen shot reprinted with permission from Microsoft Corporation and Tucows International, Inc.)

To find a suitable server, go back to the main listing of program types as shown in Figure 5.5 (p. 100) and find the heading for "Server Daemons." A "daemon" is defined as a spirit being in pagan mythology. The use of this term reflects some programmer's playful nature, because he or she is using this term to refer to a program that quietly sits in the background just waiting to perform its assigned task. When called upon, it springs forth to do your bidding and then returns to its silent vigilance. Aren't these programmers clever folks?

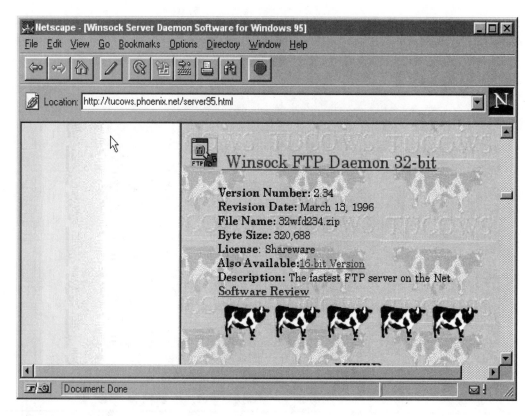

Figure 5.7 (Screen shot reprinted with permission from Microsoft Corporation and Tucows International, Inc.)

As before, when you click on this heading, you will go to a site with a listing and evaluations of FTP servers. Although there are certainly numerous candidates, our recommendation is based on ease of use, and the speed of transfer. Figure 5.7 displays that choice. Note, however, that this is a shareware program so if you decide to use it regularly, you should register and pay the small fee to its creator.

These two programs will certainly get you started on your way to transferring files across the Internet. As you become more experienced with the Internet in general, you will likely return repeatedly to this site (or others) to acquire additional software. The acquisition and use of such software, however, does entail some ethical obligations, and we will turn our attention to two of these in the concluding section of this chapter.

THE ETHICS OF USING FTP

We believe there are two primary admonitions that should concern you when you engage in file transfer across the Internet: (1) timing your transfers, and (2) paying for your shareware. We will briefly discuss each of these issues.

Timing Your Transfers

The Internet is a busy place. With millions of e-mail messages, Web pages requests, and file transfers, traffic across the Internet is multiplying on a monthly basis. Not surprisingly, with this much traffic, occasional bottlenecks or other trouble spots can slow the Internet to a crawl. The best way to avoid these slow downs is to refrain from making large file transfers at peak hours of use, from 11:00 AM to 5:00 PM (Eastern time) on weekdays.

These are the "peak" hours because they are the times when the entire country is at work and on line. If you attempt to transfer a sizable file during this time, be prepared for a lengthy wait. The system is so busy that your transfer has to compete for access to network lines and gateways, sometimes resulting in tremendous slowdowns during these hours.

This does not mean, however, that you should not engage in your daily computer business. Send your e-mail, do your Web searches, and transfer small files, but remember that even these operations will tend to be slower during this time. Similarly, there are instances when you *must* transfer a large file during peak hours. Do it if you have to, but be prepared to wait.

If you're the one doing the waiting, why (you might ask) do we present this as an ethical issue? The answer is simple: so is everybody else. This is analogous to driving 30 mph on an interstate highway. Sure, you're supposedly the only one that is driving slowly, but in reality you slow down everybody else because they have to deal with your behavior.

If everyone followed our simple advice and used the "off-hours" to transfer files, the traffic during peak time would lessen considerably. Hence, if you choose to FTP a large file during prime time, you affect us all in a negative way. That, we believe, is an ethical issue.

A second concern about timing is the overload that so much traffic brings to various Internet sites. Frankly, this is not so much a problem with commercial sites (for example, Microsoft), because they have the resources to handle such extraordinary loads. Other sites, however—particularly university sites—are not so well funded that they can expand to meet an ever-increasing demand. Many popular sites such as these, therefore, limit users during the day to keep the load off their computers.

In contrast, these sites are wide open during the evening and, especially, in the early morning hours. We are not naïve enough to suggest to college students that they do their file transfers at 5 o'clock in the morning. We don't and we don't expect you to either. But how about 9:00 AM or 8:30 PM? Virtually all sites will let you log in at those times, and the Internet will be carrying much less traffic. Chances are that you'll complete a transfer in one-third to half of the time. Something to think about.

Paying for Shareware

We have discussed the concept of shareware several times, so this is really a review and reminder: *If you continue to use shareware after a reasonable trial period, you are ethically required to pay for it.* This isn't a surprise to anybody, and you know it is the right thing to do.

Beyond the ethical dimension, if most people didn't pay for the shareware they obtain, how long do you think the (usually self-employed) programmers who write it could continue to produce these excellent programs? Considering that they must feed themselves and their families, the answer is "not long." How long would you continue to create a product if no one paid for it?

Given how little these programs cost and how useful they are, you should view them as a bargain, even on your college budget. Better yet, see whether you can talk your university into getting a site license for all students. Your fellow computer users on campus will thank you, and the shareware programmers will be ecstatic.

CONCLUSION

In the last several chapters we have discussed acquiring information of various types, e-mail Web pages, file transfers, etc. In the next chapter, we will cover two important points to consider after you have obtained that information: (1) how do you evaluate its quality? and (2) how do you appropriately cite the author or creator of that material in your report or paper?

CHAPTER 6

Acknowledging and Citing Information from the Internet

Once you have experimented with searching for material on the World Wide Web, you will realize how much easily available information exists about almost every topic imaginable. In this chapter, we will discuss some of the steps you need to take to use that information in your academic work.

EVALUATING ONLINE INFORMATION

One of the main appeals of the Internet is its accessibility. Anyone with an Internet account can mail or post messages to listservs and newsgroups around the world. Server space for individuals is now widely available. Most schools and Internet service providers set aside computer resources for personal Web pages, and publishing these personal Web pages has never been easier. Writing the code for Web pages may seem difficult, but HTML (HyperText Markup Language) is actually rather simple, once you learn the style. And, most common word-processing programs can now convert regular documents into HTML, so the entire Web publishing process can be as simple as typing a term paper. With access to a scanner, along with graphics and sound software, even multimedia is a breeze.

This accessibility brings special problems to those who use information from the Internet—namely, how to evaluate the quality of the information you discover. Again, our advice is straightforward: *You should never assume that information is accurate or credible just because you found it on the Internet.* Most of the information that we encounter when we search traditional sources has passed through many gates, or stages of evaluation. Editors of reference works and scholarly publications consult experts in various fields to determine the value, utility, and accuracy of a work before it is published. Journalists check and double-check their work. Professionals decide which books, magazines, and journals will be archived in libraries. Most traditional information resources pass through stringent screening procedures to ensure that they are accurate and trustworthy.

Gatekeeping is uncommon on the Web. If online messages are screened (as in moderated listservs or newsgroups), it is usually done to keep out flames or unwanted contributions, like **spam**. Some Internet providers screen to eliminate material that might be offensive, such as drug-related or sexually oriented content. To our knowledge, besides electronic journals, online news sources, and librarians who create information directories, there are no professionals paid to ensure that only accurate, complete, and unbiased information gets on the Internet. *Just because something is online does not necessarily mean it is accurate or credible.*

It is dangerous to assume that Internet resources are as reliable as traditional ones. One good illustration concerns the spread of misinformation about the July, 1996, crash of TWA Flight 800 off Long Island, in which 230 people died. Pierre Salinger, former journalist and press secretary to President Kennedy, was passed a "secret government document" about the crash; he claimed that he had found proof that the crash was caused by "friendly fire." He further asserted that the investigation was a smoke screen to hide a massive cover-up. Salinger's stature led his claims to be widely and respectfully reported. The information upon which he based his claims, however, appears to be bogus.

Richard Russell, a former pilot and crash investigator, later explained that he was the author of Salinger's "document." He had sent it off as private e-mail shortly after the crash, and as can happen, it was quickly forwarded in other e-mail, posted to various newsgroups, and even faxed to some newsrooms. Although Russell claims that his information is credible, he has offered no further documentation or corroboration. Subsequent investigations have shown that Russell's and Salinger's claims have no factual basis.

Perhaps Salinger was duped. Perhaps he didn't thoroughly investigate the source of his "document." Perhaps he did not realize how easy it is to post something on the Internet. There is a lesson here for each of us: Before you use the information that you've gathered from the Internet, you must first evaluate its accuracy and credibility.

Standards/Criteria for Evaluating Electronic InformationStandards for Evaluating Info

There are no special techniques for evaluating online information. Simply use the same criteria that you would use for traditional resources.

Who Is the Source of the Information? Remember that any information is only as good as its source. Credible sources are those who are experts in their chosen field. Ask yourself whether a source has the training, ability, or experience to be knowledgeable about the topic. For example, which of these sources would be more credible for data about computer ownership and WWW use: the A. C. Nielsen Company's Web site or a term paper about computer use posted by a high school student from Colorado? The A. C. Nielsen Company's Web site is probably a credible source regarding computer ownership and WWW use, because of their expertise and experience as a major television rating firm.

Credible sources are also trustworthy. Ask yourself whether the source has any reason to be biased. Which of these sources would be more credible about a senator's voting record: data from his or her opponent or data from an independent nonprofit organization such as Common Cause? Both have the resources to gather accurate data, but the opponent probably has a vested interest in slanting the information to put the incumbent in the least favorable light. So use that sort of information with caution.

Question immediately any anonymous information. Our advice is to discard any information without a verifiable source. In rare cases, however, anonymous information can offer intriguing leads. In that case, follow the example of the *Washington Post* reporters who broke the Watergate cover-up, Woodward and Bernstein. Use anonymous information *only* when it can be verified independently by other sources.

Are the Data Primary or Secondary? Secondary information is information that was gathered from other sources and summarized. Secondary sources are useful when you are trying to get some background information or an overview of a field, but these sources are not entirely reliable. Secondary sources synthesize and interpret. So if you rely on secondary sources, you are depending on someone else to draw conclusions for you. Try to rely instead on primary sources.

The availability of primary source information is one of the strengths of the Internet. It is becoming easier to find the primary data to answer most questions that you will have. For example, if you are preparing a speech about the implications of the new digital television standard, you can go directly to the FCC's Web site to read the primary documents about the decision. You can supplement that information with material drawn from secondary sources, such as newspaper and magazine articles. If you are writing a paper about tobacco company liability trials, you can go directly to the archives of the tobacco company documents. Use those primary data (http://www.library.ucsf.edu/tobacco) to evaluate the tobacco industry's claims. With the Internet search engines at your fingertips, there is no reason to rely on secondary sources.

How old is the information? Because files rest so unobtrusively on servers, much information on the WWW goes untended. Once you've surfed the Internet, you'll notice that many Web pages have not been updated since they were first posted. For some data, recency is not important, but other data must be current to be useful. For example, a list of the 50 highest grossing movies of all time would be of little value if it had not been updated since 1995, because it would not account for the three immensely popular movies released during 1996 (*Independence Day*, *Twister*, and *Mission Impossible*) and the 1997 re-release of the *Star Wars* trilogy. Consequently, you must determine how current the information is. Look for a "last updated" notation on the Web page. If the page isn't dated, try a few of its hyperlinks. If some are no longer working, that's a sign that the information may not be up to date.

There is a danger in the wide availability of electronic resources. Because the Internet can be so easily accessed, at any time of the day or night, and because you can go online from the comfort and convenience of your own home and office, you may be tempted to rely solely on the Internet for information. Right now, this would be a mistake. Online information may be sufficient for some topics and for some assignments, but you should not ignore more traditional means of research. Most communication journals are not yet available online, so if you intend to explore the primary research of our field, you'll need to go the library. A wealth of Web sites has been created by fans of old-time television. Still, nothing beats actually watching the old programs themselves. Think of the Internet as just another resource in your research repertoire.

DOCUMENTING AND CITING ONLINE INFORMATION

After you have evaluated the information that you find on the Internet, you will probably want to use it for some of your course work. And if you do, you will need to document the source of that online information for your oral and written assignments. Because widespread use of the Internet as an information resource is still relatively new, academia has not yet decided upon a single standard for citing online sources. We will draw from several resources to suggest the best ways to document these sources. But before we begin, let's briefly discuss why documentation and citation are so important.

There are three reasons for citing and documenting sources in your academic work. The *first* reason is that citation allows the credibility of the data or evidence to be established. Because any information is only as good as its source, it is important that the source of any information be documented in your work. With a citation, you demonstrate the breadth of your own research and allow your audience to judge for themselves the strength of your arguments. Citation and documentation let your audience know whether you have used primary or secondary data and the range of the sources that you have relied upon. So, a citation must include enough information to allow the audience to assess the credibility of your sources.

The *second* reason for citing and documenting resources is to give credit to others for their words or ideas. Using another's work without giving proper credit is plagiarism, a form of academic dishonesty. There is no shame is using others' ideas and published works as the basis for your class assignments, as long as you give credit to the original authors. Remember, appropriate citation strengthens your own work because it lends it the credibility of the original scholars. A student enrolled in an introductory communication class might write a paper discussing the value of knowledge in effective communication. Think how much stronger the paper would be if it drew on Berger and Calabrese's uncertainty reduction theory (1975), instead of relying solely on that student's own thoughts and impressions.

A *third* purpose for citing and documenting sources is to allow members of your audience to retrieve the same material themselves, should they wish to learn more about the topic or to double-check your work. Most systems of academic citation are designed to provide all available information about the location of printed or other hard-copy resources. Online resources are difficult to cite and document, however, because the Internet is constantly evolving: new sites and Web pages are added daily. If one of the goals of documentation and citation is to lead the audience to the original source, this may not be possible when we use online resources. Existing Web sites and pages are modified or disappear. As you search the WWW, you will frequently encounter almost blank pages that simply state "The requested URL was not found on this server." Or you may read "I've moved. Reset your bookmarks to http: . . . ." Files and users move around the Internet as people graduate and leave their schools or change their Internet providers.

Citing online sources, then, involves a trade-off. The Internet is much more easily accessible than hard-copy resources, but the locations are less permanent. The American Psychological Association (APA) suggests a compromise in the 4th edition of their publication manual (published in 1994): "If print and electronic forms of the material are the same, a reference for the print form currently is preferred" (p. 218).

Following are several suggestions for citing online sources. These are adaptations of the preferred forms of the two most common publication styles:

American Psychological Association (APA) and the Modern Language Association (MLA). For more complete information about citing electronic and online sources, visit some of the citation URLs on this book's Web page (especially the APA's own page) or check out the second edition of Li and Crane's (1996) *Electronic Style: A Handbook for Citing Electronic Information.*

APA Style

The basic form for all APA-style non-print citations is:

Author, I. (date). <u>Title of work</u>. [Medium]. Location of Publisher/Producer: Publisher/Producer.

Adapt this form for different on-line resources. The APA also suggests including the date that the material was accessed.

Books or Documents

Gaffin, A. (1995). EFF's guide to the Internet (v. 3.0). [On-line]. Available: http://caboose.com/a1topics/INTERNET/GUIDES_AND_HELP/EFFGUIDE/

Journal Articles

Newhagen, J. E., & Rafaeli, S. (1996). Why communication researchers should study the Internet. <u>Journal of Computer-Mediated Communication</u> [On-line serial], <u>1</u>(4). Retrieved April 22, 1997 from the World Wide Web: http://www.usc.edu/dept/annenberg/vol1/issue4/vol1no4.html

Magazine Articles

Noah, T. (1997, April 21). Why is TV in a jury room? <u>U.S. News</u> [On-line magazine]. Retrieved April 22, 1997 from the World Wide Web: http://www.usnews.com/usnews/issue/970421/21medi.htm

Newspaper Articles

Richtel, M. (1997, April 19). TV-type ads emerge on the web. <u>The New York Times</u> [On-line newspaper]. Retrieved April 22, 1997 from the World Wide Web: http://www.nytimes.com/library/cyber/week/041997advertising.html

Archived Listserv or Newsgroup Messages

Bowne, P. S. (1997, April 20). Re: Feminist science (references-long). soc.feminism [On-line newsgroup]. Available: feminism-request@ncar.ucr.edu

E-mail

Remember that one purpose of citation is to allow others to find the works that you have used. If you cite personal communication, or a conversation or correspondence that is not available to the public, there is no public repository for that information. So personal communications are not listed in reference lists. They are, however, cited in the text. For example, if you wanted to cite a personal communication from one of the authors of this book, you would present the information and include the following: (J. A. Courtright, personal communication, April 10, 1997). The same holds true for electronic correspondence. If the correspondence is not archived or publicly recoverable, simply cite e-mail as personal correspondence. You would not include the e-mail address of the source for the same reason that you would not include the phone number of another personal source.

MLA Style

The basic form for all MLA-style non-print citations is:

Author's last name, Author's first name. "Title of Work." *Title of Complete Work, if citation is from a chapter in a larger work*. Date: Pages or length in paragraphs. Type of on-line material. Available: Online address.

      The fourth edition of the MLA style manual (1995) also recommends that the citation be followed by the date that the source was accessed.

Books or Documents

Aristotle. *Metaphysics*. Trans. W. D. Ross. Online book. Available: gopher:// gopher.vt.edu:10010/02/39/12. 22 Apr. 1997.

Journal Articles

Bielefeldt, Heiner. "Muslim Voices in the Human Rights Debate." *Human Rights Quarterly* 17 (1995): 587-618. Online. Available: http://muse.jhu.edu/journals/ human_rights_quarterly/v017/17.4bielefeldt.html. 22 Apr. 1997.

Magazine Articles

Stephenson, Wen. "You Say You Want a Revolution?" *Atlantic Unbound* 2 Apr. 1997: 15 pars. Online edition of *Atlantic Monthly*. Available: http://www.TheAtlantic.com/atlantic/atlweb/media/ws970402.htm. 22 Apr. 1997.

Newspaper Articles

Hentoff, Nat. "The New Political Correctness." *Washington Post* 19 Apr. 1997: 16 pars. On-line edition. Available: http://search.washingtonpost.com/wp-srv/WPlate/1997-04/19/028L-041997-idx.html. 22 Apr. 1997.

Archived Listserv or Newsgroup Messages

Clinton, William J. "Remarks by the President at the Teacher of the Year Awards Ceremony, April 19, 1997." 21 Apr. 1997. Online posting. CRTNET (Communication Theory and Research Network). Available: CRTNET@psuvm.psu.edu. 22 Apr. 1997.

E-mail

Again, many of the adapters of MLA style for online resources recommend including the e-mail address of the source of any electronic communication, but we do not recommend that sources' personal addresses be included in reference lists. We recommend, instead, that students follow the MLA style for citing personal interviews:

Perse, Elizabeth. E-mail to the author. 22 Apr. 1997

CONCLUSION

Remember that the World Wide Web is another tool for you to use in your academic and professional career. Think of the Web as a giant virtual library. Develop your online search skills and learn how to evaluate the material that you locate. Make the Web your own personal library, but use it as you would use any other resource—critically and carefully.

GLOSSARY

address book

A feature of e-mail programs that lets the user store frequently used e-mail addresses.

anonymous FTP

A service for obtaining files from remote computers over the Internet. It allows the user to log on without establishing an account. Users may log on as "anonymous" and use their e-mail address as the password.

asynchronous

Communication between computers that does not require that both users or computers be on-line at the same time. Asynchronous communication also implies that computers can deal with multiple requests for information at the same time.

attachment

A file that is attached or added to an e-mail message. It is not included as part of the message text, but remains a separate file that can be saved and used by the receiver's computer applications.

binary files

Files that have been created by computer applications or programs. They are called "binary" because they exist in binary format, which is made up of series of zeroes and ones. These files contain codes or instructions that include formatting instructions, special characters, and graphics and are not readable without using the program that created them.

BITNET

Abbreviation for Because It's Time Network. An early network of IBM mainframe computers that is separate from the Internet. While it still exists and is still used, it is being phased out.

bookmark

A pointer to a specific location on the Internet that is stored by a Web browser. This feature allows users to return easily to bookmarked Internet locations without having to retype the URL.

boot sector virus

Viruses that reside in the "boot" or start-up information of computers. Boot sector viruses become active when an infected disk is used to start the computer.

browser

The software that is used for navigating and viewing files on the Internet. The best known browsers are Netscape Navigator and Microsoft Internet Explorer. A browser is a type of software that transforms a computer into a client for navigating the WWW.

client

A computer that contacts and requests, receives, and displays files and data from another computer. Clients use software that allows them to communicate with servers that send a variety of different protocols.

command-line

The line on the computer screen where the user types in commands. The command-line is usually important only in text-based Internet environments, like telnet and gopher.

digest

A listserv setting that collects all of the day's messages and sends them together only once a day. Digest reduces the amount of e-mail a user receives from a listserv.

DNS

The abbreviation for Domain Name System.

domain name

The unique name that identifies an Internet site. The form of a domain name is two or more parts separated by dots. Moving from left to right, the parts of the domain name go from smaller units to larger units, from specific to general.

download

To transfer data or files from a server to a client.

electronic mail (e-mail)

Widely used Internet service that allows users to exchange written messages over the Internet.

encrypt

The procedure that encodes computer data so that they can be read only by authorized users or recipients.

FAQ

Pronounced "fack." An acronym for Frequently Asked Questions. FAQs are lists of answers to the most commonly asked questions on a particular subject. These lists are publicly available to save time and keep experts from having to answer the same questions again and again.

finger

Internet software that allows users to obtain information about other users, such as whether the user is currently logged on and when they last checked their mail. Because the finger command looks for accounts by both a user ID and a real name, it is a good source for finding out someone's e-mail address.

flame

E-mail messages that contain strong language and are meant to criticize or provoke. A series of flames is called "flame wars."

folder

Part of the PC and Mac virtual filing systems. A folder is an organization of files. Like a manila file folder, a computer folder contains files and other folders that serve similar functions.

freeware

Software that can be downloaded, used, and redistributed at no cost.

file transfer protocol (FTP)

The set of rules by which files are copied and moved from one computer to another across a network or via a direct connection.

FTP

The abbreviation for File Transfer Protocol.

gopher

A text-based system of information available on the Internet. The gopher protocol preceded the World Wide Web. Gopher servers display menus that organize different categories of information. When users find documents that interest them, they can read, print, or have those documents e-mailed to them. Gopher was developed at the University of Minnesota whose athletic teams are known as the "Golden Gophers."

header

The top of any e-mail message that displays the e-mail address of the sender and recipient, the addresses of anyone to whom the message was copied (CC:), and the subject of the message as supplied by the sender. The header is like the "envelope."

home page

The first page of any Web Site. Also, the Web site that automatically loads each time a browser is launched.

HTML

The abbreviation for Hyper Text Markup Language.

HTTP

The abbreviation for Hyper Text Transfer Protocol.

hyperlink

A connection within one Web document to another. Clicking the mouse on the hyperlink alerts the browser to move to the URL embedded in that hyperlink.

hypertext

A computer document that contains hyperlinks to other documents. Hypertext documents allow users to follow many paths through and across documents, by clicking on hyperlinks.

hypertext markup language (HTML)

The computer language or code that creates hypertext documents for the World Wide Web. Browser software translates the code to control the placement and appearance of text, graphics, and multimedia objects.

hypertext transfer protocol (HTTP)

The set of rules and routines used on the World Wide Web to request and supply Web pages.

in-box

The e-mail folder or directory that stores incoming e-mail messages. Most mail programs have in-boxes that display a list of received mail by sender and subject (as supplied by the sender).

Internet

The global network of computers connected to each other that use TCP/IP protocols to transfer data.

Internet Protocol (IP)

The protocol that manages data communication between computers on the Internet. Internet protocol uses a unique address for each computer that is marked by a series of numbers separated by periods called "dots" (e.g., 128.175.30.73).

Internet Relay Chat (IRC)

Text-based real-time conversations on the Internet. IRC sites are servers that simultaneously handle many different "channels" or on-going conversations. Users read text entered by other users and type their contributions from their own terminals.

IP

The abbreviation for Internet Protocol.

log on

A series of commands that establishes a connection to a host computer.

lurk

To read messages on a listserv or newsgroup without posting. This is a good way to get the "feel" of the discussion before entering it.

Mac

Refers to a MacIntosh computer.

macro virus

Viruses that attach themselves to programs that use templates to create documents. When the templates or macros are used, the virus is activated.

mailbox

A folder used by an e-mail program to store mail messages. Common mailboxes are the in-box and out-box. Mail programs allow users to customize and create new mailbox folders.

mainframe

A large computer that is designed for heavy use by multiple users. Mainframe computers can handle many tasks concurrently.

MILNET

An early network of mainframe computers used by the military (Military Net).

multimedia

Using computers to combine and present text, images, audio, and video.

Net

Informal term for the Internet.

nickname

A short, easy-to-remember name that stands for a longer e-mail address. Nicknames are useful tools for e-mail because they are easy to remember and save key strokes.

out-box

For most mail programs, the out-box holds copies of outgoing messages that have been sent. A few programs use the out-box to temporarily hold out-going messages until they are sent.

PC

Abbreviation for personal computer. Usually refers to any IBM-compatible computer.

platform

The basic computer system defined by hardware and software. Common platforms are the (Windows-based) PC, Macintosh (Mac), and Unix.

protocol

The set of rules that allows computers to be networked, or connected so, that they can transfer and share data.

search engine

A program on a Web server that performs and returns keyword searches for documents that have been posted on the web.

search string

Key words or phrases that are entered into search programs and become the basis of an Internet search.

server

A computer that responds to clients by providing access, data, and files to other remote computers.

shareware

Computer programs that users are allowed to try before purchase. Much shareware can be downloaded from the Internet.

signature

A file used by e-mail programs that contains a few lines of text that identify the user. Signature files usually contain personal information; typically the user's name, snail mail address, and phone and fax numbers. E-mail programs automatically attach the signature file to each outgoing message. Using a signature file saves time and key strokes.

spam

Junk e-mail or mass postings to listservs and newsgroups, usually containing commercial messages.

synchronous

Communication between two users or computers that requires both to be online and communicating at the same time. With synchronous communication, each exchange must be completed before another is initiated. Synchronous communication can be contrasted to asynchronous communication.

telnet

An Internet protocol that allows users to use their own computer as a remote terminal to a host computer. Telnet allows users to interact with the remote host as if they were logged on locally. The most common uses of telnet are database searching on remote hosts and checking e-mail.

thread

A collection of newsgroup postings or articles that all deal with a common topic. A thread is made up of the initial posting and all responses to it.

troll

Posting messages on newsgroups or listservs that are designed to agitate readers. Trolling is like baiting others to participate in a counterproductive discussion.

uniform resource locator (URL)

The "address" of any file that is on the Internet.

UNIX

Pronounced "you-nix." UNIX is a mainframe computer operating system that began at Bell Labs in the late 1960s. UNIX is the underlying software that runs the computer and all of its programs. It is analogous to DOS or Windows on PCs. UNIX is the system that is used to write most of the protocols that run the Internet.

URL

Pronounced "you are el." The abbreviation for Uniform Resource Locator.

uudecode

The most common program used to translate binary files that have been attached to e-mail on UNIX systems. Uudecode converts a binary file (graphic, text file, sound file, or program) to and from ASCII. In its ASCII form, the file can be attached, sent, copied, and moved, but if viewed it will look like gibberish until it has been decoded.

virus

A computer program that is attached to other programs and spreads itself as the host program is run. Most viruses are merely annoying, but a small number are destructive and can corrupt files, erase data, or cause computer systems to slow down or crash.

the Web

Another term for the World Wide Web.

webmaster

The person who creates and maintains a Web site.

the World Wide Web

That part of the Internet that uses hypertext transfer protocol to deliver files from server computers to client computers. The World Wide Web uses a computer language called hypertext markup language to mix text, graphics, audio, and video.

WWW

The abbreviation for the World Wide Web.

APPENDIX

Useful Communication Bookmarks

Search Engines

   MetaCrawler Searching
   http://metacrawler.cs.washington.edu:8080/index.html

   HotBot
   http://www.hotbot.com/

   WebCrawler Searching
   http://webcrawler.com/

   Alta Vista: Main Page
   http://altavista.digital.com/

   Archie Request Form
   http://hoohoo.ncsa.uiuc.edu/archie.html

   Listing of Listservs Worldwide
   http://www.tile.net/listserv/

   FTP Interface
   http://hoohoo.ncsa.uiuc.edu/ftp/

   DisInformation
   http://www.disinfo.com/

   Electric Library
   http://www.elibrary.com/id/2525/search.cgi

Dogpile
http://www.dogpile.com/

OpenText
http://index.opentext.net

Excite
http://www.excite.com/

Lycos
http://www.lycos.com/

Information Directories/Web Guides

Yahoo
http://www.yahoo.com/

Infoseek
http://guide.infoseek.com/Home?page=Home.html&sv=N3"

Web Ring Directory
http://www.webring.com/

INTERNET—Directories
http://www.december.com/cmc/info/internet-directories.html

Look Smart
http://www.looksmart.com/x02/

CNET SEARCH.COM
http://www.search.com/?nscp

SEARCH.COM–desperately seeking someone you know
http://www.search.com/Seeking/Someone/

Switchboard—Search for People's Phone Numbers
http://www2.switchboard.com/

Webcrawler
http://www.webcrawler.com

Galaxy
http://galaxy.einet.net

Journalists' Source List
http://www.mediasource.com/Links.html

White & Yellow Pages

Phone Directory for Universities
http://fiaker.ncsa.uiuc.edu:8080/cgi-bin/phfd

Bigfoot
http://www.bigfoot.com/

GTE SuperPages
http://superpages.gte.net/

ONVILLAGE
http://www.onvillage.com/

WhoWhere?
http://www.whowhere.com/

World Pages
http://www.worldpages.com/

Find a Person
http://www.switchboard.com/bin/cgiqa.dll?MG=

Four11 (e-mail directory)
http://www.four11.com/

E-mail directory
http://www.555-1212.com/

Pine Information Center
http://www.cac.washington.edu:1180/pine/

Email: WhoWhere?
http://www.whowhere.com/

E-Mail Web Resources
http://andrew2.andrew.cmu.edu:80/cyrus/email/

Internet Address Finder
http://www.iaf.net/

INTERNET—Searching—People
http://www.december.com/cmc/info/internet-searching-people.html

Find a Person
http://www.switchboard.com/bin/cgiqa.dll?MG=

Yellow Pages
http://yellow.com

Yellow Pages Unbound
http://www.bigyellow.com

The 1991 Zipcode Guide
http://www.usps.gov/ncsc/aq-zip.html

AT&T Toll-Free Internet Directory
http://www.tollfree.dir.att.net/

1-800 Directory
http://att.net/dir800

Reference

General

Internet Public Library
http://ipl.sils.umich.edu/

The Skeptic's Dictionary
http://wheel.ucdavis.edu/~btcarrol/skeptic/dictcont.html

Speechwriters Bookshelf
gopher://gopher.arcade.uiowa.edu:2270/0F-
1%3a35095%3aSpeechwriters%20Bookshelf

Welcome to the Top of the Web
http://www.december.com/web/top.html

FAQs by Category
http://www.lib.ox.ac.uk/internet/news/faq/by_category.index.html

Hypertext Webster's Dictionary
http://c.gp.cs.cmu.edu:5103/prog/webster

On-line Reference Works
http://www.cs.cmu.edu:8001/Web/references.html

On-Line Ready Reference
gopher://sol1.solinet.net/11/On-Line Ready Reference

Dictionaries etc
http://galaxy.einet.net/galaxy/Reference-and-Interdisciplinary-
Information/Dictionaries-etc.html

Biographical Dictionary
http://www.mit.edu:8001/afs/athena/user/g/a/galileo/Public/WWW/
galileo.html

Barron's Guide to On-line Bibliographic Databases
gopher://riceinfo.rice.edu/1ftp%3aftp.utdallas.edu%40/pub/staff/
billy/libguide/

Virtual Law Library Reference Desk
http://lawlib.wuacc.edu/washlaw/reflaw/reflaw.html

The World Wide Web Virtual Library
http://lcweb.loc.gov/

On-Line Reference Works
http://www.cs.cmu.edu/Web/references.html

Webster's Dictionary
http://www.en.utexas.edu/studentresources/referencedesk.html

Roget's Thesaurus of English Words and Phrases
http://home.thesaurus.com/thesaurus/

The Virtual Institute of Information
http://www.ctr.columbia.edu/vi/

An Electronic Library of Classic Text
gopher://chico.rice.edu/11/Subject/LitBooks

Dictionaries
http://galaxy.einet.net/galaxy/Reference-and-Interdisciplinary-Information/Dictionaries-etc.html

Reader's Guide
http://sawfish.lib.utexas.edu/~beth/Tour/readersguide.html

All-in-One Site Improved
http://www.dreamscape.com/frankvad/home.html

Metric Primer
http://www.dot.ca.gov/hq/oppd/metric/metrictoc.html

Hypertext Webster Interface
http://c.gp.cs.cmu.edu:5103/prog/webster?

Biography Resources
http://www.tiac.net/users/parallax/

APPLICATIONS—Information—Library
http://www.december.com/cmc/info/applications-information-library.html

APPLICATIONS—Communication—Mass
http://www.december.com/cmc/info/applications-communication-mass.html

The Social Science Information Gateway
http://sosig.esrc.bris.ac.uk/

Internet Public Library
http://ipl.sils.umich.edu/

The World-Wide Web Virtual Library: Statistics
http://stat.ufl.edu/vlib/statistics.html

My Virtual Reference Desk
http://www.refdesk.com/

Research It
http://www.iTools.com/research-it/

Background Briefing
http://www.backgroundbriefing.com/

In Reference
http://www.cs.uh.edu/~clifton/macro.a.html

Project Gutenberg
http://www.promo.net/pg/

Communication Resources

Journal of Computer-Mediated Communication
http://www.usc.edu/dept/annenberg/journal.html

Communication Institute for on-line scholarship
http://WWW.CIOS.ORG/

Communications Scholars
http://alnilam.ucs.indiana.edu:1027/sources/dirpage.html

CMC—Mass
http://www.december.com/net/tools/cmc-mass.html

CMC Information Sources—Level 3 TOC
http://www.december.com/cmc/info/toc3.html

ACA Social Science Communication Research Collection
http://cavern.uark.edu/comminfo/www/social.science.html

Media History Project
http://www.mediahistory.com/

Virtual Institute of Information (telecommunications, mass media, and cyber media)
http://www.ctr.columbia.edu/vi/win_index.html

Film and Television Studies
http://eng.hss.cmu.edu/filmtv/

Media and Communication Studies
http://www.aber.ac.uk/~dgc/medmenu.html

Communications Central
http://www.govst.edu/commcentral/

Academic Communication Sites Around the World
http://www.jou.ufl.edu/commres/jouwww.htm

American Communication Journal
http://www.uamont.edu/~adams/acj.html

Museum of Broadcast Communications
http://www.neog.com/mbc/

ERIC

ERIC (Educational Resources Information Center)
gopher://ericir.syr.edu/1

ERIC Clearinghouses (Syracuse)
gopher://ericir.syr.edu/11/Clearinghouses/16houses

ERIC/Reading, English, Communication
http://www.indiana.edu/~eric_rec/index.html

Quotations

Quotations
http://www.xmission.com:80/~mgm/quotes/

LoQtus Quotation Resource Page
http://pubweb.ucdavis.edu/Documents/Quotations/homepage.html

Bartlett, John. 1901. Familiar Quotations
http://www.columbia.edu/acis/bartleby/bartlett/

CHA's Quotations about change
http://www.cha4mot.com/quo_chng.html

CHA's Quotations about Communication
http://www.cha4mot.com/quo_comm.html

CHA's Quotations about ideas
http://www.cha4mot.com/quo_idea.html

CHA's Quotations about invention
http://www.cha4mot.com/quo_invt.html

CHA's Quotations about vocation
http://www.cha4mot.com/quo_voca.html

CHA's Quotations about life
http://www.cha4mot.com/quo_life.html

Style Sheets

APA Frequently Asked Questions
http://www.apa.org/journals/faq.html

Guide to Style Manuals
gopher://iliad.lib.duke.edu/00/DULib_Res/Bibliographies/
STYLEMAN.HO

Network-Based Electronic Publishing of Scholarly Works
http://info.lib.uh.edu/pr/v6/n1/bail6n1.html

Basic Legal Citation
http://www.law.cornell.edu/citation/citation.table.html

The MLA-Style Citations
http://www.cas.usf.edu/english/walker/mla.html

Grammar and Style Notes
http://www.english.upenn.edu/~jlynch/grammar.html

Guide for Citing Electronic Information
http://www.wilpaterson.edu/wpcpages/library/citing.htm

Guide to Citing Government Information Sources
http://unr.edu/homepage/duncan/cite.html

MLA-Style Citations of Electronic Resources
http://www.cas.usf.edu/english/walker/mla.html

MLA Citation Guide
http://www.cas.usf.edu/english/walker/mla.html

MLA Guidelines to Evaluating Computer Related Work
http://jefferson.village.virginia.edu/mla.guidelines.html

Web Extension to APA style
http://www.nyu.edu/pages/psychology/WEAPAS

Web Extension to American Psychological Association Style
http://www.nyu.edu/pages/psychology/WEAPAS/

Electronic Sources: MLA Style of Citation
http://www.uvm.edu/~xli/reference/mla.html

Electronic Sources: APA Style of Citation
http://www.uvm.edu/~xli/reference/apa.html

APA Publication Manual Crib Sheet
http://www.gasou.edu/psychweb/tipsheet/apacrib.htm

Walker/ACW Style Sheet
http://www.cas.usf.edu/english/walker/mla.html

Bibliographic Formats for Citing Electronic Information
http://www.uvm.edu/~xli/reference/estyles.html

Classroom Connect: REVISED How to Cite Internet Resources (10/96)
http://www.classroom.net/classroom/CitingNetResources.html

Copyright

Media and Telecommunications Policy and Legislation, Copyright and Intellectual Property Information
http://www.lib.berkeley.edu/MRC/MediaPolicy.html

Fair Use
http://www.libraries.psu.edu/avs/fairuse

The Copyright Website
http://www.benedict.com/

SUL: Copyright & Fair Use
http://fairuse.stanford.edu/

Copyright Management Center
http://gold.utsystem.edu/OGC/IntellectualProperty/cprtindx.htm

ILTweb5: Projects: Copyright Guide: Index
http://www.ilt.columbia.edu/projects/copyright/index.html

Bacal's Legal Sites
http://www.azlink.com/lawyers/

KuesterLaw Technology Law Resource - Patent Copyright Trademark
http://www.kuesterlaw.com/ index.html

Wellesley College Copyright Policy
http://www.wellesley.edu/Library/copyright.html

Multimedia Product Dev.: Clearing Rights
http://www.batnet.com/oikoumene/nobomediarights.html

Government Resources

Thomas—Legislative Information on the Internet
http://thomas.loc.gov/

U.S. Government hypertexts
http://sunsite.unc.edu/govdocs.html

U.S. State Department
http://www.law.cornell.edu/

Federal Election Commission
http://www.fec.gov/

Federal Communications Commission
http://www.fcc.gov/

White House Briefing Room
http://www.whitehouse.gov/WH/html/briefroom.html#fsbr

Office of the Director of Central Intelligence
http://www.odci.gov/

United States Postal Service
gopher://www.usps.gov:80/hGET%20/

US Statistical Data
http://www.stat-usa.gov/

Government Statistics
http://www.fedstats.gov/

U.S. Government Printing Office
http://www.access.gpo.gov/

Statistical Abstract of the United States
http://www.census.gov/stat_abstract/

Smithsonian Institution
http://www.si.edu/

National Science Foundation
http://www.nsf.gov/

U.S. Government Documents and Publications (NU)
gopher://toby.scott.nwu.edu/1D-1%3a2652%3a04.fed.docs
849289734 0 0

Federal Register (Counterpoint)
gopher://gopher.counterpoint.com/1

Factbook on Intelligence (CIA)
http://www.ic.gov/facttell/toc.html

United Nations Web Server
http://www.un.org/

U.N. Scholars Workstation
http://www.library.yale.edu/un/unhome.htm

Related Organizations
http://www.unsystem.org/index.html

U.S. Postal Service
http://www.usps.gov

U.S. State Department's Travel Advisories
http://www.stolaf.edu/network/travel-advisories.html

Tax Code Online
http://www.fourmilab.ch/ustax/ustax.html

Library of Congress Web
http://lcweb.loc.gov

IRS Digital Daily
http://www.irs.ustreas.gov/prod/cover.html

Government Information
http://www.access.gpo.gov/su_docs/aces/aces760.html

GPO Access
http://www.access.gpo.gov/su_docs/aces/aaces002.html

Federal Budget
http://ibert.org

FedWorld
http://www.fedworld.gov/

PIPER Resources
http://www.piperinfo.com/~piper/state/states.html

Local Government Web
http://www.localgov.org/

City.Net
http://www.city.net/countries/

Union of International
http://www.uia.org/website.htm

Federal Government Agencies
http://www.lib.lsu.edu/gov/fedgov.html

Communication Organizations

AEJMC
http://www.aejmc.sc.edu/online/home.html

Radio and Television News Directors Foundation
http://www.rtndf.org/

American Association of Public Opinion Research
http://www.aapor.org./

Broadcast Education Association
http://www.usu.edu/~bea/

Society for Technical Communication
http://stc.org/

Encyclopedia of Associations
gopher://gopher.cic.net:2000/11/e-serials/archive/alphabetic/e/eoa

Scholarly Societies: An Electronic Guide
http://www.lib.uwaterloo.ca/society/overview.html

Society of Professional Journalists
ftp://ftp.netcom.com/pub/spj/html/spj.html

ICA Home Page
http://www.io.com/~icahdq/ica/ica.html

Speech Communication Association
http://www.scassn.org/

WSCA - Western States Communication
http://www.csufresno.edu/speechcomm/wsca.htm

SSCA - Southern States Communication
http://www.uamont.edu/~adams/ssca.htmlx

SCA Undergraduate Student Organization Page
http://cotton.uamont.edu/~roiger/scaclub/start.html

American Communication Association WWW Archives
http://www.uark.edu/depts/comminfo/www/

Legal/Law Resources

Findlaw Internet Legal Resource
http://www.findlaw.com/

Individual Rights in America
http://asa.ugl.lib.umich.edu/chdocs/rights/Citizen.html

Criminal Law Links
http://dpa.state.ky.us/~rwheeler/

Cornell's Legal Information Institute
http://www.law.cornell.edu/

News and Current Events

New York Times
http://www.nytimes.com

Washington Post
http://www.washingtonpost.com

Editor and Publisher
http://www.mediainfo.com

Links to Newspapers and News Services
http://www.newslink.org

An Internet news service
http://www.newspage.com

USA Today
http://www.usatoday.com

Wall Street Journal
http://www.wsj.com

Christian Science Monitor
http://www.csmonitor.com/

Online newspapers
http://marketplace.com/e-papers.list.www/e-papers.home.page.html

C-SPAN Gopher
gopher://c-span.org

World News
gopher://gopher.nstn.ca/11/Cybrary/News/news

VOA Current News
gopher://gopher.VOA.Gov/1/newswire

The Electronic Newstand
http://www.enews.com/

Radio Tower
http://www.radiotower.com

Newslink
http://www.newslink.org

Newspage
http://www.newspage.com

Reuters
http://www.reuters.com/

PBS Newshour
http://www1.pbs.org/newshour/

Microsoft Network
http://www.msnbc.com

Fox News
http://www.foxnews.com

Weather Channel
http://www.weather.com/

Court TV
http://www.courttv.com

Television and Radio Sites

Radio Stations
http://www.brsradio.com/stations/

TV Stations
http://tvnet.com/tv/us/stations5.html

National Public Radio
http://www.npr.org

Radiospace
http://www.radiospace.com/

CBS
http://www.cbs.com

ABC
http://www.abc.com

NBC
http://www.nbc.com

CNN
http://www.CNN.com/

C-SPAN
http://www.c-span.org

VOA
http://www.voa.gov

WB
http://www.tv.warnerbros.com/

UPN
http://www.upn.com/

ESPN
http://espnet.sportszone.com

FOX
http://www.foxnetwork.com

PBS
http://www.pbs.org

TV resources
http://www.ultimatetv.com/

Discovery Channel
http://www.discovery.com

Turner Networks
http://www.turner.com

First Amendment — Free Speech

Banned books On-line
http://www.cs.cmu.edu/People/spok/banned-books.html

MediaScope
http://www.mediascope.org/mediascope/

Media Watch Dog
http://theory.lcs.mit.edu/~mernst/media/

Project Censored
http://censored.sonoma.edu/ProjectCensored/

Call Them On it (Telecommunications)
http://www.callthemonit.com/

Electronic Frontier Foundation
http://www.eff.org/

Center for Democracy and Technology
http://www.cdt.org/

ACLU
http://www.aclu.org/

Fairness and Accuracy in Reporting
http://www.fair.org/fair/

Free Speech Issues
http://www.xnet.com/~paigeone/noevil/noevil.html

Freedom Forum First Amendment Center
http://www.fac.org/

General Internet Resources

Frequently Asked Questions

Index to FAQ sites–Good Resource!
http://ps.superb.net/FAQ/

Welcome Newbie
http://www.netwelcome.com/index.html

E-mail Resources

FAQ: Finding e-mail addresses
http://www.cis.ohio-state.edu/hypertext/faq/usenet/
finding-addresses/faq.html

Beginner's guide to Effective e-mail
http://www.webfoot.com/advice/email.top.html

Remailer Information
http://electron.rutgers.edu:80/~gambino/anon_servers/anon.html

HTML Resources

Compendium of HTML Elements
http://www.synapse.net/~woodall/html.htm

HTML Goodies
http://www.htmlgoodies.com/

Newsgroups and Listservs

Reference.Com
http://www.Reference.COM/

Tile.net (Listserv and Newsgroup Resources)
http://www.tile.net/

Liszt Mailing List Directory
http://www.liszt.com/

Usenet FAQ
http://www.ou.edu/research/electron/internet/use-faq.htm

INDEX

FAVORITE WEB SITES

Name of Site: _____

URL: _____

Name of Site: _____

URL: _____

Name of Site: _____

URL: _____

Name of Site: _____

URL: _____

Name of Site: _____

URL: _____

Name of Site: _____

URL: _____

Name of Site: _____

URL: _____

Name of Site: _____

URL: _____

Name of Site: _____

URL: _____

Name of Site: _____

URL: _____

Name of Site: _____

URL: _____

Name of Site: _____

URL: _____

Name of Site: _____

URL: _____

Name of Site: _____

URL: _____

Name of Site: _____

URL: _____

Name of Site: _____

URL: _____

Name of Site: _____

URL: _____

Name of Site: _____

URL: _____

Name of Site: _____

URL: _____

Name of Site: _____

URL: _____

Name of Site: _____

URL: _____

Name of Site: _____

URL: _____

Name of Site: _____

URL: _____

Name of Site: _____

URL: _____

Name of Site: _____

URL: _____

Name of Site: _____

URL: _____

Name of Site: _____

URL: _____